In Time & Motion

Edited by Steve Twelvetree

anchorbooks
Poetry by the People
for the People

anch**o**r books

First published in Great Britain in 2006 by:
Anchor Books
Remus House
Coltsfoot Drive
Peterborough
PE2 9JX
Telephone: 01733 898102
Website: www.forwardpress.co.uk

SB ISBN 1 84418 422 6

Foreword

Anchor Books is a small press, established in 1992, with the aim of promoting readable poetry to as wide an audience as possible.

We hope to establish an outlet for writers of poetry who may have struggled to see their work in print.

The poems presented here have been selected from many entries, and as always editing proved to be a difficult task.

I trust this selection will delight and please the authors and all those who enjoy reading poetry.

Steve Twelvetree

Editor

Contents

The Poems

Continuing The Tiger's Stripes

The elephant trumpeted, *stop that noise*
Lifted his trunk and struck a poise
But all he could now hear
Was the growl of the bear.
Just everyday sounds
Like the howl of the hounds,
The monkeys' chatter
Also their patter,
The leopard was growling too
I've got plenty of spots, enough for two.
Who ever had stolen the tiger's stripes?
Perhaps they were hidden in the pipes?
The hyena laughed with his horrible cackle,
Kangaroos were ready for battle.
The gates got locked at five and opened at two,
No other animal could enter the zoo,
The giraffe looked around
And guess what he found?
Outside the zoo in a field with cattle,
The snake, you know the one with the rattle?
A chimpanzee in a frock
My! oh my! what a shock!
What else did he see?
He could hear a noise like a bumblebee,
A queer animal with a mane.
Another with stripes, was he insane?
Not a bit like a tiger,
Or anything else either.
They were all jumping and jigging about:
A man with a trumpet thing, giving a shout.
It was a carnival, giving a show
When it was over, tiger got his stripes back
So all's well that ends well
And the show was enjoyed by all.

Phyllis Wright

Trespassing

When I was a boy and a naughty boy,
I played by the railway line.
I'd place my coins upon the track,
Watch them spring and fly right back,
Against bare shins they'd sometimes slap
When I was a naughty boy!

When I was a boy and a naughty boy,
I'd go and watch the trains.
At level crossing I would hide,
In the woods by the homeward side,
Telling myself I never lied
When I was a naughty boy.

When I was a boy and a naughty boy,
I put my ear down to the rail,
I heard the loco chugging down line,
Freight or passenger - balance fine,
Then I knew they were running on time
When I was a naughty boy!

One day I put a threepenny bit
On the line to flatten it,
The loco gave a sudden kick
And I was away to the woods so quick
And I was a naughty boy!

The level crossing on the bend,
Distance signal on long white pole,
When all was quiet up there I stole,
In summers good, in winter cold
And I was a naughty boy!

Plate-layer's hut along the track,
No lock on door, so in I crept,
Frightened a tramp who in there slept,
I ran so fast, but never wept
And I was a naughty boy!

Under Bull Lane bridge there stood a house
With iron blast doors it was cast,
Secrets of the war just passed,
Boys' adventures here could last
When I was a naughty boy!

Once curiosity laid me flat,
Detonators by the track,
I poked at them, they poked me back,
Leaving face and hands all black
And I was a naughty boy!

To the station I would repair,
Taking my engine numbers there,
Two friendly drivers that I knew
Took me on as extra crew
And on the footplate, there I flew
And we were all such naughty boys!

When I was a boy, I hadn't a care,
I played all day and did my dares,
I drove the engines of my dreams,
Never came to harm it seems
Though I was a naughty boy!

Graham K A Walker

An Ordinary Man

This is the story of an ordinary man, born in eighteen ninety-four;
A quiet, kind, gentle man, a countryman to the core.
He was born on a farm, the youngest of six,
Four girls and just two boys,
He learnt the ways of the countryside, but the horses were his joys.

When he reached eleven, he left school because he got a job
Doing the thing he loved best in the world
And it paid him a couple of bob!
For he became groom and coach-boy for the people up at the hall;
Sometimes after work he'd be so tired,
He'd sleep with a horse in its stall.

When fourteen he signed indentures and became apprentice to
The local blacksmith - the obvious choice -
For that's what he wanted to do.
And just as he finished his seven years, the war broke out and so
He joined the Royal Engineers and off to war did go.

He followed his trade, caring for horses, the transport of that war;
He became a sergeant and served in France,
But never told what he saw!
But he was there at the battle of the Somme and later at Verdun,
At Ypres and then at Passchendaele where
The mud and the swamps won.

His bravery went on record, but he kept that to himself . . .
He very quietly got on with the job . . . his medals just put on the shelf.
After the war, he worked on the mines - a farrier caring for horses
And helping on his father's farm for they needed all their resources.

For the next ten years this handsome man was the beau at every ball,
He was strong yet gentle, with an impish quick wit
And he was loved by all.
At thirty-five he met the girl who was to change his life . . .
She was twelve years his junior but he knew right away
She was to be his wife.

They married in nineteen twenty-eight, a time when life was hard;
The mine closed down, his father retired, their happiness was marred
By lack of work, of money, of food, but never a lack of love,
He scraped a living from the land and they thanked their God above.

A daughter was born after fourteen months
To make their lives complete,
And they both 'went without' to feed and clothe her
And put shoes on her feet.
And with the great depression over,
The hunger marches were no more,
He got work making steel for Dorman and Long
And he worked on the furnace floor.

For the next few years their life was good, they even went on vacation,
But storm clouds were gathering and very soon
War was to hit the nation.
His work, making steel, was vital for all and he laboured
Twelve hours each day
For seven days a week, without a day off . . . what more can one say?

He proudly gave his daughter away in marriage in fifty-four,
His son-in-law became his best friend:
He couldn't have loved him more
And then they gave him two grandchildren
Who brought him endless joy,
He loved them both so very much, his treasures, a girl and a boy.

He retired when he was sixty-six,
But retirement knocked him off course,
Doing his garden just wasn't enough, so he found a job with a horse.
A gentleman's groom, it suited him well, for he was a gentle man,
Both horse and rider respected him, and so a new chapter began.

But tragedy struck in sixty-nine when his wife suddenly died . . .
For forty-one years they'd never been parted,
She was always by his side . . .
Yet he was always the first to say, 'God's been good to me . . .
My life has been blessed in so many ways,' his gratitude plain to see.

He'd always been fit and enjoyed good health
And so it came as a shock
To learn that his lungs were beyond repair;
The cancer was firm as a rock.
He was paying the price of working in the mines
And on the furnace floor,
Inhaling the industrial dust and the poison gas in the war!

But he faced his illness as they knew he would
With courage and dignity,
Always cheerful, always a smile and grateful sincerity.
Concerned for his carers, not wanting to be a trouble or cause a fuss,
His doctor said, 'One in a million - a model for all of us.'

On July the ninth in seventy-three his life came to an end
And everyone who'd known him knew they'd lost a friend . . .
And the world became a sadder place,
But I'm sure those in Heaven were glad,
And I'm proud to say that ordinary man was my beloved Dad.

Betty Brown

The Great Exploiter

The dog, we say, is man's best friend,
For master and home he'll defend,
But man's best friend - workwise of course
Till modern times has been the horse.
Though man's been no friend in the least
To this manipulated beast.
Throughout mankind's grim history
This fine creature, born to run free.
Has frequently been harshly used,
Overworked, beaten and abused.
With brutalness that should appal
We've held this noble beast in thrall;
Forced iron bars between his jaws
And spurred him into bloody wars;
Condemned him to a man-made hell;
Torn his flesh with sword, lance and shell;
Driving him on till his last breath
To an excruciating death.
In more recent, enlightened times,
We immured him in Hadean mines,
Down in a subterranean hole,
Blindly dragging truckloads of coal.
Kept in the bowels of the Earth -
Nevermore to tread soft green turf.
This is the way man treats dumb friends,
Exploiting them for his own ends.
Could any philosopher refute
That man has been a callous brute?
Deny that one of our worst creatures
Is the way we use other features?
Though perhaps that's not surprising -
Really doesn't need surmising,
When we see, as we daily can,
The way man treats his fellow man!

Arthur Allen

Changing Scenes

Hearing again that wonderful hymn, in my late autumn days
'Through all the changing scenes of life'
      What memories of life's many changing ways
Remembering happy schooldays, wondering what would
      the future hold?
My reading, writing and reckoning was not too bad
      'You'll do all right,' so I was told
I didn't need what I'd learnt in school
      The first real job I had
At fourteen working on a coppersmith's forge
      Sums and poetry were not much help, 'Keep the bellows
      going lad.'
The first year remembering lines
      someone else had put together
The smith a mighty man is he, this to me
      was not quite true however
He did have broad and sinewy hands
      and swung his hammer with real skill
To my surprise he didn't know about Milton, Tennyson or
      Shakespeare. He couldn't read I remember still.
Two years and then the smith said,
      'We don't need you anymore.'
I wish my teacher had been there
      what had he filled my head with poetry for?
Poetry was not going to feed or clothe me or give any help
      with life's problems I might need
The depressing headlines of the twenties didn't worry Smithy
      He couldn't read.
The next few years the changing scenes were not
      always for the better.
I roamed the country unemployed, living in digs
      and hostels, then in Sheffield I had a letter
There was a chance that back in Bristol
      I could go and learn a trade
Home again, the decision not too difficult that I had made
      My reckoning, not my poetry, was to serve me in good
      stead
Those long division decimal sums were still clearly in
      my head

Reading plans and operation drawings to me became
      an easy task
The foreman said, 'If there is anything you don't understand,
      just ask.'
Five years and then I had a title, I'd become
      a skilled universal miller.
That changing scene, I always knew there was a
      special someone at the tiller
Then the romantic changing scene, I wed and
      became a family man
Building a humble home together that brought a love
      that only a wife and children can.
Then many changing scenes, the clouds, the tears,
      that left vacant chairs
Still in my loneliness I say, 'Why Lord?'
      in my prayers.
The changing scenes are plentiful. I could go on and on
      But time is short I must not dwell here too long
I still think about the poetry I learnt
      was it all a waste of time?
I suppose it did help me to learn to write in rhyme
      I've read that he who makes a garden
      helps to make the world a better place
I cannot make a garden now though I sometimes
      fill an empty space
With words our Lord has given me to bring a little pleasure
      Remembering now the changing scenes with all of you
Dear Lord in my autumn years, I have so much to treasure.

Fred Norgrove

Danby Old Mill

One night I sat beside the stream
That fed the water mill
And soon I fell into a dream,
For all the world was still.

An owl sat hooting in a tree
In a thicket nearby.
The mill is now a ruin
And is open to the sky.

I thought of all who toiled there,
Some sixteen hours a day
And cap in hand, went to the boss,
To collect their meagre pay.

And did they go out poaching,
Or fish the old mill stream?
And would they be quite happy
With chub or perch or bream?

How else could they have managed
On such a lowly pay?
And would they hide a bag of flour
When the miller was away?

And would they use the herbs to smoke
From plants that grew nearby?
And make the drugs to ease their pain,
When they were going to die?

And did they, when they were ill,
Their lungs all choked with flour,
And underfed at forty-odd,
Then reach their final hour?

What happened to their wives
And the families that they fed?
Did they simply move away
To find their daily bread?

I wonder if their spirits lurk here
In the dead of night.
Does a restless miller walk
In dusty, ghostly white?

And does a man walk round,
To check the belts are tight?
And have a pot of grease in hand
To make the cogs work right?

And will a ghostly cat appear
To chase the ghostly rats?
Or are their spirits living on,
In the form of owls and bats?

As I walk a little further
Down the eerie moonlit track,
And feeling rather nervous,
Just keep on looking back,

I ponder all the questions,
But I'm never going to know,
Just what life was like at this old mill,
Four-hundred years ago!

D B Bowes

Mammy

Mammy
Will ye always
Be there when I need
The Germelene and bandages
To clean me
When I bleed?
If my heart gets broken
Can you put it right?
If I have a fever
Will you soothe me
Through the night?
If I call you
When I leave home
Will you make time for me?
If I turn up
Without notice
Will you forgo the old TV?
As you get on in your years now
It seems that we talk more
It's always nice
To see your face
When you answer the door
By asking you these questions
That might to you seem slight
It's just my way of keeping in touch
To make sure you're alright
I know we've had our ups and downs
But they are a long time passed
I've always had you in my thoughts
Whatever came to pass
I'm your first born baby
Now at fifty-one
I still recall my childhood
As one of such great fun
We never had much money
I know that things were tight
But you gave us
What you can't buy
A childhood of delight

The future is not definite
So what will be, will be
Mammy you are everything
In life
Precious to me!

Kevin Raymond

To My Special Someone

Scared to love, scared to trust
Am I just company with an element of lust?
A victim again I'm scared to become
My feelings emerge slightly, then again they fall numb

I say the words yet I fear they fall on deaf ears
Been searching for that unconditional love for far too many years
Just when I think I've found it, it shatters like precious glass
And I wonder why I feel that I'm forever living in my past!

I make people see the person I want them to see
Yet they never know the depth of pain within the *real* me
Too scared to tell the story, the horrid sordid truth
Would anyone really believe me without solid given proof?

I've never known what it's like to live just what it's like to survive
And I still keep at bay that girl inside who wants to come alive
I know she's still there within me, but she's just too afraid
To trust another person for fear of being betrayed

'Do you really love me?' is always my question
Needing constant reassurance for the fear of that rejection
I always feel I'm never good enough yet I yearn for that acceptance
Is it possible for someone to love me without so much subjection?

I feel sorry for some of the people I meet along my way
The ones I always push away when really I want them to stay
I'm not sure how to solve that, it's like it's terminal with me
A cancer slowly killing me deep inside that you cannot see

I'm looking for a way out so it doesn't hurt me anymore
How to trust that special someone that my heart wants to adore
Yet it's just too hard for me to believe life can be kind
It's all life's cruel lessons and how they just won't leave my mind

But if I'm writing this to you then I guess it shows I am willing to try
How I really want to believe that you won't ever say goodbye
I feel very lost at the minute but I don't know how to
                              make you understand
How I feel inside and my fears of what future life has planned

Anchor Books – In Time & Motion

I'm just asking you for patience and endurance of my insecure ways
And just a little reassurance at times that would bring sunshine

to my days

It's not the big things that matter to me, it's the little ones you see
I'm sure that is all that's needed to heal the real me.

Esta Taylor

Temptation

Who is this evil knight, who moves in the night?
Who shines like a light, but ain't heavy, is he light?
Who comes to befriend and blend though he pretends
He tends to con, put it together - he contends

You think he brings peace, until he offers you a piece
Comes to your herd and says haven't you heard
It's not how you think it is, sit and have a drink
There is nothing wrong with this, know what I mean, *wink, wink?*

When you should be kneeling down at the altar
He comes up with an idea, so then you alter
Your stand, cos you don't really understand
So you fall for nothing like your legs were made from jam

Now I think about the times I was magnetised and enticed
By lies and eyes and thighs, devised
For my demise I compromised and did not realise
To my surprise I was unwise by this sin disguised

As something good that I would, or even should, embrace
There you stood strong like wood with a smile on your face
Friendly as ever, therefore I endeavoured
Not being too clever it changed my life forever

I felt the guilt of a criminal, so down I wore a frown
A king without a crown I was looked upon like a clown
Is the news around should I leave town?
Will they come and surround, hunt me down with hounds?

I feel as bad as it is, but man look at this
My so-called brother, so-called sister, chatting my biz
In the church I overheard, the way that they slurred
So absurd but it occurred, so bad but that's the blurb

What you sayin' bruv? Hi Sam, faking the love
So now you're listening and thinking that I'm above
You call me judgmental and regimental
I speak the truth from my heart, so check your mental

Lessons for life, the storm transformed
Me from the norm to no longer conform
But informed me and reformed me so that I may perform
In a fitting way, so listen to what I say

Temptation will come every day
From the month of June to April and May
Temptation may come to the brays, from girls like June, April or May
When you're supposed to be working, there's a desire to play
Always feel like going when you're supposed to stay

Samuel Martin Jnr

The Onward Journey Of Endurance

My love is like a shipwreck,
Lying dead upon the ocean shore,
Abandoned, broken into pieces,
She lies there maybe for evermore.

As once she ruled the ocean tides,
She conquers all that has died.
She knows the stillness of the calm,
The open sky, the moon, the stars.

The gentle breeze evokes sails to glide,
Across the southern skies.
She attempts to embrace the stormy sea,
As the karmic waves arrive,
Her destiny denied.

She is ready for the abyss of sea and wind,
To enable thee to fly.
As the thrashing waves beat upon her brow,
Her sails strong against the force of the gushing gow.

Thy will ride the roughest tides,
For a notion to be free.
Braving the battle of the elements,
The passion of thy will is a need as deep as thy way,
To carry her soul to the ends of the earth.

Until the oceans turned and burned,
As her sails were set so high,
She thought that swirling winds and seas
Would pass her by.

Until they brought her down,
Leaving her high and dry,
She is helpless to the fall,
As the doves have recalled.

Her sails are broken,
The creaking of the bow doth rock.
As she breaks upon the coast
With the spirits of her storm.
As she crashes against her worlds,
Her words are spoken.

As the gentle bits of driftwood,
Float amongst despair.
Does anyone care the waves surrender for the day?
To see the turning point of May.

No, this is not the end my friend,
But the beginning to an end.
So we may start again,
For our souls to be free within you and me.

So love can start for eternity.

Millie Love

Our Family - Normal To Us!

(Based on our son with an autistic spectrum disorder)

It's often hidden but some can see it.
There's just something but you can't give it a name.
Sometimes it's visible all the time but not to everyone.
And it's not a condition where someone's to blame.

There are few who know the real meaning
And most don't know what it is when it shows.
Some people say they know what it entails
But are still overwhelmed when he blows.

If he joins in you're lucky and honoured,
But never push or attempt to co-opt
'Cause he will be watching and listening.
And if the noise gets too much, look out.

He has always been happy and polite.
He has always been loving and warm.
It just so happens that he has also done things
That are just that bit out of the norm.

He lined up his cars for the rally.
He pushed trains round the carpet in his room.
If the noise gets too much he covers his ears,
But he just loved cars on TV go *vroom*.

He watched Murray Walker repeatedly.
He loved Top Gear the best.
He got excited when cars crashed and got mangled.
Dad's PlayStation never got a rest.

All this before the age of two.
A talented child you may say.
But we never got to watch anything different.
He always wanted to have his own way.

Then a febrile convulsion at eighteen months.
Words that had started to form had now gone.
No longer did he know 'one, two, three'.
Had I imagined his speech all along?

Anchor Books – In Time & Motion

I asked the health visitor about his welfare.
She said, 'give it six months,' I said, *'No!'*
I know my own child - he needs help *now*.
Six months is too long not to know.

So she referred him and we got him some help.
Eventually referred to a wonderful team.
At seven he still can't look at cereal with milk
Or someone else eating ice cream.

So why have I never been bothered
When others stare at the child by my side
And when they tut and speak behind me
Why do I now take it all in my stride?

It's partly because this child is my son.
The most special, the most amazing, creation on Earth.
My son was *born* with this condition
That I know has been visible since birth.

My son has an *autistic spectrum disorder*.
His sensory issues are specific but bizarre.
He has to know where we are going all the time
And insists on a specific seat in the car.

He attends a special language unit.
With their support and their help he is great.
We have fought to get him everything
'Cause no one tells you what you can get from the state.

I am positive in my outlook for his future.
He was my first child and will always be so.
And his younger sister loves him unconditionally.
It's magical watching them grow.

See to her, he is just Ruaridh,
Her brother, who goes out to play but gets upset.
She loves him and loves to play with him.
They often play at being each other's pets.

They both stress us out daily,
My daughter probably more than my son.
They both are full of energy
And definitely know how to have fun.

I am delighted my son has great opportunities.
We have moved house to get the support he will need.
Mainstream school is within his grasp now.
I hope others will set good examples and lead.

Ruaridh has got some friends in our new street,
They all moved in within a few weeks of us.
Ruaridh is learning to play with others.
And trying really hard not to make a fuss.

He has been out playing since we moved to this new house
And would never leave my sight without telling me where
And has started using his scooter
Which Santa brought him last year.

One day he just jumped on his bike without stabilisers.
I tried not to startle him with my shock.
He just got on the bike and started cycling
And is now as steady as a rock.

He asked one day to do ballet and drama,
Two hobbies where he is a star,
So we enrolled him in groups this summer
And is proving that he will go far.

Some say I am lucky that his condition is so mild.
That his tendencies now are not so apparent.
But to us he is simply our dear Ruaridh.
We are so glad that we are his parents.

So a few tips when life gets a bit stressful:
Learn to laugh at their funny little ways.
Never take anything for granted.
And take lots of photos on good days.

I thank you for reading my poem.
If it helps anyone out there I am glad.
I am positive and will remain focused
And will never ever be sad!

Alicia McLean

Our Day Out In Dorset

The aroma of garden lavender
As the path led away from the lane
Then over the stile to the meadow,
It was good to be in Dorset again.
A small flock of sheep were grazing
As we studied the map where to go,
The sun was warm in the valley,
Our enjoyment was beginning to grow.

The bramble-lined path was a challenge
But we were set on reaching our goal,
This walk was lifting our spirits,
Undeniably feeding our soul.
The butterflies danced about us,
Intent on what they had to do,
Sensing the abundant thistle,
Flowers of the brightest purple hue.

We followed a fork to the right,
Up so steep, we climbed steps to the top,
Feeling the heat increasing,
I paused, giving my brow a mop.
Then beyond the cliff we saw
A wonderful, stunning view,
A clear summer sky displaying
A sparkling sea of blue.

Waves hammered the rugged coastline
As we looked down over the edge,
From west to east we turned
And recognised Dancing Ledge.
A rest on the grass we relished
As we watched distant yachts sail by,
It's easy to love this green pleasant land
And days like this are why.

Pat Williams

We Have To Say Goodbye

So, that was my life,
How did it end?
Did I leave willingly?
I couldn't have.
Did I get a chance to say goodbye?
I hope I did.
Did we leave any words unspoken?
Have no regrets.

Did I ever hurt you?
Please forgive me.
Did I love you?
Then you must have deserved it.
Was I there when you needed me?
I wanted to be.

Are you glad that you knew me?
Then speak of me with fondness.
Were you ever kind to me?
Then I thank you.
Did you love me?
I tried to deserve it.
Have I really left you?
My love could never leave you.

Shani Clarke

So Poverty Can Dance

'Tis the music that is Africa
With lyrics written not by chance
Whose song is set before the world
On which poverty does dance

The song tells a cynical story
On a stage of many screens
A rhythm that once was beautiful
That now feeds the tortured dreams

Being once the cradle of humanity
The womb where life did breed
Now used as a second-hand artefact
By the spirit of human greed

Exploited by the lost generation
And raped by its very kin
Leaving only the immortal sadness
Of a continent abused by sin

Disease and famine roam its plains
Preying on the young and weak
Contaminating all who cross the path
Where now only ghosts do meet

And upon the wind came music
The song sings of civil wars
But for once the chorus tells
Of hope sitting on other shores

Hope sings with a choir of angels
The present hears not a word
But deep within the African soul
Is a song that can be heard

Though memories that sung of yesterday
Are kept in a political trance
For fate still choreographs the lands
So poverty can dance.

David Bridgewater

And Death Shall I Be?

I

And death shall I be

In all with none
As felled drops of time, into endless
Caves of sorrow
Stretched by the longing
Of love's touch
Seeking without pause
A sleep

And death shall I be

For I having taken
By the wild sketcher's leave
A savage path
Now find myself at ease
Accepting fate
And in fact urging it to skeleton fair
Its chalk, slender outlines
Of me

And death shall I be

On a river's breath
As dust, to blow cool beyond
And far past
Her midnight lips, searching
Tongue
And perfect eyes
Perfect
Perfect eyes
From these and yet worse
I shall be free

And death shall I be

For all I possess
Is and is not a thing of such
Since you
Oh daughter of Persia
Clasped my hand
And pointing it up high
Hung the sky jewels
Somewhere, between my heart
And your eyes

In death I shall be

II

And death shall I be?

When you call
A howling clown of sighs
I kneel

Pulse at foot
Shall I, the black gown kiss?
Accept all I fear
And be still evermore?

Yes . . . I will cut
And draw you, the vulture's scent
To weave, weave
Weave me
A fine gown, loneliness
In shadow's bliss
I will

Rise
And take you naked
By the throat
And crush
Together
To blackless dust
Eternal
And laughing
Forever

Death, I shall be.

Sache

Voices In The Wood

Here in the old wood,
Where it is never bright day,
There is no silence.
The trees rustle and click;
The hedges susurrate;
Birds chatter;
But there are more unidentified voices than that.
It is a very old wood.

The people came often long ago
From the village in the valley.
They trudged here to work and manage,
To prune and saw and gather.
It was a peaceful place:
Work is peaceful.
But, hundreds of years back,
The people went away -

And so did their village.
You can barely see its traces now -
Just a few stones,
Blackened patches in the meadow
As if the grasses remember
And are circumspect.
There are more signs of those ancient folk
Here in the darkness of the wood -

A gully here, a platform there;
Something rustling in the thicket;
Clear signs of a paved track.
And softly amid the visible evidence
That they were here,
The unidentified sounds
Press soundlessly upon the ear,
A tuneless song beyond singing.

Busy it is on the road.
But down by the banked ditch
On the huge shiny log,
Which has not grown mossy
In all that time,
The sounds are peaceful.
You can hear the snatched kisses
And soft sibilance of sin.

No one comes here any more.
Why would they when
It is so overgrown and dark?
But perhaps each one of the wood folk
Left some part of himself behind
To carry on abstracted
And eternal conversations
With the trees.

Ted Harriott

Forever Fields

Through childhood days I'd go to sit, run and play in fields
Through ever changing seasons.
Memories of autumn walks, for me the face of fields were new,
Exciting hues of foliage spread endlessly across their vast expanse
With a richness only they possess.
How still the air, I hear her voice and Mother Nature speaks to me,
Her colours plead, 'Please notice me, my days are nearly over,
My last attempt to shine for you with gifts left me from summer.'
Winter's teeth bit short bland grass through which my carefree feet
so easily ran -
Smiles of joy and happy heart,
Downhill with freedom I would fly so fast with feet that barely touched
the ground -
I'm sure the angels carried me . . .
Sweet music lulled me to the steam where tinkling fairy voices
softly sang,
Sunshine smiled on priceless gems beneath the liquid glass,
I reach and thirst to touch its sparkling face
With frozen fingers skimming through the crystal ice -
Its waters spill her stardust on my skin.
These pastures trodden by ancient Man,
Renewed once more by spring's fresh kiss,
Tipped with frost, new shoots and blossoms
Proudly unfold their virgin bodies towards an irresistible light.
Rejoicing swallows noisily return to nest in the land they love and
know so well
Befriending lambs, I jump and play with fluffy white mischiefs on velvet
green around spring's emblem, the ever faithful daffodil.
My world is born again.
Blessed summer skies of bluebell blue,
Loyal its duo the scorching sun,
Rays of warmth and love shed out on all its thriving kingdom.
I sat and watched life's picture book.
Old Father Oak in all his years has sheltered and shaded along
life's way.
But somehow his branches sway and say,
'This summer is more perfect than the one before.'

Wild flowers celebrate their burst of beauty, fragrantly flirting with
a passing bee,
Their vivid colours show off in all their splendour.
Singed manes and tails adorned sunbathing mares,
Lazily grazing amidst carpets of sun drenched buttercups
Unworried by their offsprings' plight.
A flash of foals' chestnut frenzies past preceded by teasing butterflies
provoking playful kicks;
They wince and race in hot pursuit -
Perhaps they're chasing sunbeams . . .
Scenes to savour and growth at its summit,
I linger on in the lush green grass,
Dark fruits of the season plump and succulent upon my tongue,
Graced by the unforgettable blackberry.
Gentle breezes passed by whilst sweet aromas filled my head
With wafts of new mown hay from further fields,
In those golden days of summer.
And now the years have carried me through cares and scenes of life,
I take my children back to play where I possessed such happiness
In what seems like only yesterday:
I hear their shouts and screams of glee, as I remember well -
In years to come, 'Oh greenest pastures please remain
To give them back themselves as you have done for me.'
I lie on earth and feel its strength penetrate my very being,
Filled with exultation my soul elates -
My senses are alive with life,
'Oh Lord! I thank you for this land, it never fails to give me back
my core!'
I chase my spirit to the sky,
Alive with hope I lift my arms and pray to God,
That they will always be -
                              Forever fields.

Fiona George-Veale

Summer Solitude

Behind me the chalk wall rose stealthily
Like a cloud of smoke over the faded heads of the linseed,
Wrinkled poppy seeds drooping in isolation on the edges of fields
Leading down to the silent gardens of Alciston.

Walking away from the village across the stubble wheat,
My boots scraping lazily, rhythmically,
Over the tops of the dry, thin stumps,
Some fields already ploughed over
And empty of their tidy bales,
Which only last week had stood
Like huge counters on a carpet of land
Sweeping up to the distant foot of the downs,
I could now see the dust spread up into the air
From the machines cutting their neat squares and odd circles
Across the rolling uneven farmland.

Below the church slope at Berwick,
The spire signalling to me
And watching me for miles from its wooded mound,
Great rolls of hay sat on trailers,
The sun lighting up the now drab yellow strips of earth.

I'd left the church there suddenly last week
When disturbed among the peace
Of the medieval stones and the bright modern murals.

So, yesterday, again in Folkington
I left a couple viewing graves
And walked along the brambled path,
Climbed the stile and lost myself
In the broad sweep of the meadow
Drifting like a wave below
The hillside filled with August's
Flush of violets, purples
And the light blue of forget-me-nots
And the red clover in tall grasses,
All richly thrust up by the heavy rain.

Returning to the church
And welcome emptiness I
Stood and waited in the half
Expectant gloom,
And finally drove home,
Dust falling fast
On flint walls behind me.

John Feakins

Silence

Silently and alone I often cast my eyes
Back through the maze of my life
Only now as a man do I see that which was there all along
A mother's love
Ever proud
Never judging
Always forgiving
Always loving

Through times of tears, you were by my side
When my tears fell, yours were nowhere in sight
In my times of joy, you watched so proud
When your pride-induced tears fell, I never saw them

Silent and in the background you watched me become a man

Your wisdom and strength imparted
But only now do I see and understand them both
They live on in me, and in all I do
The man I am now is because of you

Silently and alone I think of you watching over me
From wherever you are, your smile and love reaches me
It helps me through my times of fear
And encourages me to give my all

From even your deathbed your gaze held mine
And told me there and then of your love
Your pride of who I was and who I would become
Then my tears fell, and even in death you were by my side

Silently from the background I know you watch my life unfold
When fear touches my heart and mind
I feel you guiding me through the darkness
And you help the night pass into day
In times of success I feel your love shining with me

I feel your hand on my shoulder when I'm unsteady
Your love guides me to this day
And I know it always will be there

As from the silent background you watch my life unfold
Ever proud
Never judging
Always forgiving
Always loving

Your voice may be silent, but I'm never alone
In the silence I hear you talking to me
Silence is now a friend of mine
A friend who comforts me and guides me

Now a big step is nearing for me
And I wish I could get a comforting hug from you
As I ready to up sticks and move
Move on with my life, and a future with a loved one
A loved one who I know you'd love and adore
A woman who helps to mend the hurt
And fill the hole where once you dwelt
A mother's love is so complete
But the love of a possible wife to be can help to heal the pain

I'm now on a long road, which takes me to my future
And all that's missing is you to wave me on my way
As I look behind me now, I see an empty doorway
Where once you stood to either wave me off to school, or see me out
                                                                    to play
Your tears of joy and pride fell unseen even back then
But now I see only your smiling face lighting my path

Silence from the background tells me you watch my journey begin
In silence my heart tells you I love and miss you
Then silence brings your love returned
When the silence of death takes me I know you will be there
There as you always have been
With a mother's love
Ever proud
Never judging
Always forgiving
Always loving

Greg Webb

Stop And See

We take so much for granted
The things we see and hear
We look but do we see?
We listen but do we hear?

Think of those who cannot see
Whose sight has slowly faded
To those the sounds are distant
Of those who cannot hear

To live in a world of darkness
Or in a silent world
Not knowing what things look like
Or knowing how they sound

They use their hands to feel and touch
To find the beauty there
Sometimes I think they see more than we
Whose eyes can see quite clear

How do you explain the colours
Or Jack Frost on the ground?
The dew upon the rosebuds
Or the snowflakes coming down?

We take these things for granted
It is really too much bother
To stop and look and really see
The beauty of one thing or another

The patter of the raindrops
The singing of the birds
How do you explain it
To those who have never seen or heard?

There's so much beauty to be seen
If we would only take the time
Stop and take a closer look
Then you will see what I mean

Just *stop,* for a moment
Listen, and really hear
For the sights and sounds are wonderful
In this world of ours.

Joan Wright

My Dentist

'I'll take your tooth out,' he smiled, 'it is rotten
Caused by too much chocolate and rum,'
But before I could scream and leap out the chair
He'd shoved his jab into my gum

The pain of it hurt, it was crippling
My heart leapt around like a top
Then he pushed the chair down and proceeded to yank
At my tooth, but I shouted to stop

He smiled and said, 'Just relax son,
It won't take a moment to pull.'
But when the yanking was done I sat up and yelled
'You've pulled the wrong one out, you fool!'

'Are you sure?' he said looking quite stunned
'I am certain I've got the right one.'
'Don't be stupid,' I said, 'just look in my mouth
Do you take good ones out just for fun?'

'Oh dear,' said my dentist, 'I'm sorry
I see where I've made the boo boo,'
So, with his needle aloft, he shot into my gum
And pulled out tooth number two

'My God, you're insane,' I screamed in his face
'Your day for a tooth pulling spree?'
This time he just smiled, and again he jumped in
And, yes, he pulled number three

I tried to jump up but he was too heavy
He held me down and I knew there was more
As his eyes twinkled bright, and with pliers held tight
That's right! Out came number four

By now I was feeling quite faint
Would this man never stop?
Would he let me survive?
Too late. He'd pulled number five

I remembered him counting to ten
Then I fainted, but when I awoke
He was standing beside me, a grin on his face
And my teeth on a string round his throat

'Do you remember last Thursday?' he uttered
'When you emptied my bin on the path
And you let my tyres down and you spat in my face
And your friends stood around and just laughed?'

'Do you recall setting light to my front fence
And calling my mother a w****
And throwing a brick through the window
Do I have to say any more?'

I sat and I pondered a short while,
'Last Thursday this happened, you say
Well, I'll tell you right now, I was absent
On a day trip with Mum to Aunt May.'

'She lives in Southend, you can call her'
The blood in my mouth made me choke
But the dentist just stood, the blood ran from his face
He'd obviously got the wrong bloke

With the last grain of strength I could muster
I punched him, and laid him out flat
Then I picked up the needle and said, 'Open wide
This will hurt, I promise you that.'

J M Davey

The Hunted

Crashing blindly through the undergrowth
With fear and startled fury
Pursued by red dressed horsemen
Yapping dogs, his judge and jury.
On and on he gamely runs,
Terror lends him speed,
Panic stricken, scared and helpless,
Way ahead of the pack he leads.
Breath comes in short sharp gasps
And the pace cannot be held for long,
Saliva whips from his gaping mouth
And from his flapping tongue.
Outnumbered in the chase he knows
That danger's everywhere,
Bewildered, confused and frantic
He's lost the scent to his lair.

Hurry fox, oh hurry do,
Deny man his cruel blood sport,
Don't stop now, don't ease your stride,
Keep travelling or you'll soon be caught.
Dashing off in search of safety
He aims to stay alive,
Onward, onward though he's tiring,
His will is to survive.
Pumping in his winded body
His heart will surely burst,
Legs are slowly, slowly ceasing
To pound upon the rich dark earth,
Jumping, leaping over ditches,
Through the bushes and the fields,
Ripped fur, blood dripping,
The victim to his torment yields.

Now heaving body sucks for air,
The quarry has stopped his run,
Weak legs collapse from under him
The huntsman's hour has come.
But poor fox drags his weary self
Beneath the bush for cover,
With struggled breath and trembling heart
He waits, knowing life is over.
So full of fear those coal black eyes
That dart within his face,
Crouched defenceless on the ground
For death to end the race.

A shout goes up of, 'Tally-ho,'
This cry will urge each hound,
The fox has been spotted,
Prevented now his run to ground.
Horses snorting, shying, prancing,
Hounds barking, snapping for the kill,
Horn blowing drowns excited voices,
Coats as red as blood they spill.
Shouts and cries of mad emotion
As the hunted tries in vain
To cheat his captors of their folly,
But the luckless creature dies in pain.
The red decked vultures
Hold aloft the prized noble brush,
Whilst through their veins
The contents of the stirrup cups still rush.
Such sights I've never seen before
Nor wish to see again,
The victim hounded to its last
For a 'sport' that's inhumane.

Doreen E Millward

A Visit To The Vet!

She is looking at me mournfully,
Eyes pleading, begging, 'Set me free!'
I smile and gently rub her ears,
'I simply can't do that my dear.'

On her neck a raw, infected path,
Which, if let loose, she would scratch.
Hind foot armed with strong black claws
Already lifting from the floor.

A trip made to veterinarian,
Purse at the ready, yet again!
Once arrived, she starts to sing,
Rich contralto, 'What a din!'

Full throated now, Bonnie doth protest,
'Please save me from fate worse than death.'
Nice vet comes out to see the fun,
Bon greets him as a long-lost chum!

In the consulting room we confer,
A tale of pus and missing fur!
At her head I seek to distract
But she trusts no one at her back.

Soprano scream and she makes a run,
Vet in pursuit, thermometer's gone!
'Oh my God! You silly old girl!'
Clatter on floor and all is well.

Nothing daunted, vet carries on,
Clippers in hand to see what's wrong.
'Oh no,' yells Bon, 'oh not that!'
And dances around like a scalded cat.

One good thing; never shows her teeth,
But oh my back and poor bruised knees!
Vet looks up, 'I'll call the nurse,'
Tight-lipped I grin, 'She can't do worse!'

Avoiding Bon's accusing gaze,
She knows when she has been betrayed!
Emotions mixed, I leave the room,
My Bonnie girl must meet her doom!

I hear the thud, the door frame shakes,
A battle royal taking place!
An expletive? A muffled curse?
'Oh God, don't let her eat the nurse.'

Behind the door a silence falls,
A whimper escapes down the hall.
At last the upper hand they've gained
When crash! The door shakes in the frame!

Door opens wide, out comes Bonnie,
Eager; yelling, 'Where's my mummy?'
Try to disown her though I might,
Of my life, Bonnie is the light.

Matted hair lies on the floor,
Proof that vet has won once more.
Cream for morn and night I'm clutching,
To ease the itch and stop her scratching.

And so beside me she is tied
And whither I go she must bide.
Now she's pleading, wants her bed,
'But I've seen you before,' I said.

Brown eyes melting and adoring,
Forgotten all about this morning!
But if she does so much as twitch
I'll spifflicate the little bitch!

Valerie Camp

I'm The One: Lyrical Verse

I couldn't help but see
All my friends were watching her and she was watching me
We knew each other instantly
And all the loves before
And all the keeping score became a memory
It's a game of win or lose
Now the other guys wish they could stand inside my shoes
But none of them will ever understand
Uh huh
Uh huh
That's right
That's right
How it feels to be her man

The love she gives
The love she takes
A man could live on the love she makes
Every night I thank the stars above
I'm the one
I'm the one
I'm the one she loves

It's a game of win or lose
Now that I'm back in my baby's arms there's nothing left to prove
Uh huh
Uh huh
Oh yeah
Oh yeah
I've found what I've been looking for

The love she gives
The love she takes
A man could live on the love she makes
Every night I thank the stars above
I'm the one
I'm the one
I'm the one she loves

Nothing's worrying me
When I'm in my baby's arms it's so plain to see
I won't be searching anymore
Uh huh
Uh huh
That's right
That's right
I've found what I've been searching for
The love she gives
The love she takes
A man could live on the love she makes
Every night I thank the stars above
I'm the one
I'm the one
I'm the one she loves
Uh huh
Uh huh
All right
All right
All I wanna do is hold her tight

The love she gives
The love she takes
A man could live on the love she makes
Every night I thank the stars above
I'm the one
I'm the one
I'm the one she loves.

John Faucett

Dora

One hundred years
　　Have passed you by,
　　　　Where did the time go? It seemed to fly.

The sun has risen, the sun has set,
　　How many more times? You know, not yet.
　　　　From baby girl, into a young lady you grew.

When you were twenty-five,
　　The nest you flew.

A husband, a home, two children to care for
　　What more could you want,
　　　　What more could you ask for?

You sailed to the east,
　　You sailed to the west.

You've laughed and cried
　　And have been put to the test.

The years rolled by, you did your best,
Then came the time to have a rest.

All of a sudden you were on your own,
　　Having never contemplated life alone.

You don't understand
　　What's going on,
　　　　You're thinking to yourself, *has my mind gone?*

Dementia has struck and taken your mind
　　You can't have it back,
　　　　It's so unkind.

The children rally,
　　It's their turn to worry,
　　　　They do all they can and don't make you hurry.

I hope they don't think badly of me,
　　Did I make mistakes?
　　　　Do they still love me?

I can still laugh
　　And have a smile to share
　　　　If only I could tell them I still care.

I'm muddled, confused,
　　This is not fair.
　　　　No wonder I have grown - white hair.

They took me to Gallions View,
　　And said, 'Let's give it a try!'
　　　　And that's where I sit and watch the days go by.

But look, hooray, at last I'm not alone,
　　There's twenty-nine others
　　　　Like me in the home.

The years have passed,
　　And there have been lots of changes
　　　　Over periods of time and at different stages.

Memories of the past
　　Flow in and out,
　　　　What has your life been all about?

It's been great, and it's been fun.
　　And Dora you have certainly had a good run.

Anne Watson

Kittens Don't Sleep

Christmas gifts all bought and wrapped
and I am frazzled to the bone.
'White Christmas' playing on the stereo,
- the TV's blaring, 'Home Alone'.

Kittens pulling tinsel from the tree
and running throughout the house.
Why can't they occupy themselves
by chasing that ever-threatening mouse?

Too tired to go any further,
I will just call it a night.
I'll finish trimming the tree and door
by the morning's refreshing light.

Decorations, some left in boxes,
some on tables and on chairs,
candles in assorted colors,
angels to be sorted and put in pairs.

The nativity not yet completed,
the pieces lie on the coffee table.
I should finish it tonight,
though my spirit is willing, flesh just not able.
Turning out the lights,
oh to sleep, to rest.
Tomorrow will be much better,
where I can do my best.

As my head hit the pillows
I felt a thumping in the bed,
there were the kittens all three
and one landed on my head.
What a rambunctious trio,
always in some trouble, but so sweet,
each having his own identify.
'Ouch!' One just bit my feet.

Precious the little mixed grey one, the leader
was examining my stuffed up nose,
batting at my sleepy eyes,
a new game to play, I suppose.
Lovey, the black and white
sitting on my hip, posing as the winner
from some made up kitten fight.
There sat *Sweety*, the little tiger stripe
busying himself in the headboard,
finding a stray earring to chase.

Aggravating they are, but so adored.
Finally they scampered from the bed.
Ah yes . . . sweet earned sleep,
drifting . . . drifting . . . drifting off,
not a sound . . . not a peep . . .

Morning arrived all too soon,
so off to the living room, I had work to do.
'Oh my word . . .' my eyes were met
with treasure to trash from a wrecking crew.
Garlands strung from room to room
and somewhere one wise man met his doom,
the other two tending one lone sheep,
appears the shepherd boy had left the living room.
Chewy marks on candles and boxes,
ribbon and tags on the floors,
truly I see the meaning of
'when it rains . . . it pours'.

The stockings no longer hung
by the chimney with care,
decorating the carpet and under
Harley's old rocking chair.
This was a sight and let me say,
'twas not for the faint of heart.
Someone very busy, I am thinkin',
has tore the house apart.
Remote for the TV missing,
computer mouse hanging by the cord,
rearranged Christmas videos
from the desk where they were stored.

Wrapping paper off the rolls
like a colourful runner to the door,
glancing around the disaster area,
could there be even more?
But who did this dastardly deed?
The kittens were sound asleep.
Keeping a weary eye on them
I began to sweep.
Knowing it wasn't Santa
too soon for that old elf,
the dogs looked in awe
at books no longer on their shelf.

I'm thinking as the days go on
some of the proof will be seen
in spit up fur balls
of bright tinsel of blue, red and green.
Later saved by grace . . .
I surmise
by the dirt box in the bathroom,
the man, not looking all too wise?

I should hire out this lively crew
to a demolition team.
For just a can of food
they can work at full steam.

What this house needs now
is some mice for the destructive three
but complaining set aside,
they bring such laughter to the hubby and me.
Every home needs the likes of them
for you just can't be down or sad,
when you watch the kittens at play (or work)
enjoying the silly antics, what fun we had.

Merry Christmas and happy holidays
to yours from the Griffin house.
Blessings of the season from
the hubby and Lady Church Mouse.

Sandy Griffin

Anchor Books – In Time & Motion

To Terrorists

Blood-soaked sand,
Rivers of red,
Flying fragments,
Twisted tendrils,
Heat-seeking missiles,
Hurled high,
Landing in fragile flesh,
East, west, north, south,
Can anyone seek shelter?

Cowering cowardly attacks
Wrapped as warfare.
Mindless destruction
Sown in secrecy.
How is it possible
Any rational mind
Can use religion
Worshipping God,
To promote this madness?

Can we finally realise;
Many paths to one place,
One God, one Creator,
One family.

Relinquish righteousness,
Surrender superiority,
Temper intolerance,
Uphold unity,
Vanquish violence,
Without war!

Step aside,
Pray for peace,
Before it is over
For us all.

Honora G Simon

To My Birth Family

Remember me, little Gyp
Who left Dunkeld with trembling lip?
Left my home, all that I knew.
Left my litter playmates too.
Two strangers took me far away,
'Near Peterhead,' I heard them say.

I was lonely, lost and sad.
'Cheer up,' they said, 'it's not so bad,
Even though you're now alone
You'll soon make new friends of your own.
Cousin Jo has sent a Ted
For you to snuggle in your bed.'

So much was strange, so much was new.
So much to learn, so much to do.
'Wear your collar, walk on your lead,
Puddles inside we do not need.'
Would I ever get it right?
'Try hard,' they said, 'and then you might.'

'Bramble and Bracken, our elderly cats,
Still manage to catch occasional rats.
But Bramble's old and needs his rest,
Leave him alone, don't be a pest.
Now Bracken, he's still full of zest,
He loves to play and likes dogs best.'

Life became a bundle of fun,
Bracken and I were on the run.
Chasing up and down the stairs,
Falling over feet and chairs,
Until our mum got cross and said,
'Now that's enough, outside instead.'

When Bracken went to find his bed,
I played a game called 'Strangle Ted'.
Grab him by the throat and take him,
Toss him, catch him, growl and shake him.
Every time I was the winner,
Until out came poor Teddy's inner.

The neighbours said, 'My, how he's grown.
How old now? The time's just flown.
How's the training? Hmm, that's good.
Almost doing what he should.
Persevere and don't despair,
Give him time and he'll get there.'

Look at me now, all grown up,
No longer just a little pup.
I come to call and sit when told.
Mum says I'm getting very bold.
I bark at noise outside the door,
But don't jump up, stay on the floor.

The only time my dad gets mad
Is when I dig, he says, 'That's bad.
Play with Bracken, play with toys,
Play with your bone or make a noise,
But *don't* dig up my beans and peas.
Don't dig the grass or under trees.'

All in all, life's pretty sweet.
I know I've landed on my feet.
Two humans at my beck and call,
I hardly miss Dunkeld at all.
Just, now and then I dream I'm there,
A pup again without a care.

Jeanette Allen

The Acrocats

Kenny and Benny stretched out flat
The desired arrangement for a household cat
Benny's paws twitched as he lay in the sun
Dreaming of ways to have more fun
How they both craved adulation
Their names picked out in illuminations
Desiring fortune, desiring fame
Recognition was the name of their game

Suddenly the lights picked out a regal figure
Striding to centre stage with elegant vigour
The ringmaster swept off his hat and bowed
To the restless and expectant crowd,
'Ladies, gentleman, girls and boys
Thanks for your patience, now please make some noise
Welcome to the significant, magnificent act
That is Kenny and Benny, The Acrocats.'

Before the throng of eager faces
Kenny and Benny went through their paces
Soaring high upon a golden trapeze
Benny caught Kenny with accomplished ease
With bated breath they watched them fly higher
Diving through hoops ringed with fire
How the crowd roared with joy and delight
As the two cats continued their spangled flight

Suddenly Kenny awoke with eyes gleaming
Brown eyes crossed from so much scheming
No longer the model of ginger simplicity
The hair on his coat charged with electricity
Benny jumped up and down on the spot
For Kenny's idea was well, really hot
Licking a paw and winking an eye
Their dearest ambition lay very close by

The word spread to cats far and near
(Cats have fine senses; it was easy to hear)
That there was to be a show of breathtaking skills
With juggling, balancing and associated thrills
So gathering at the appointed time and date
(To be near the front they could not be late)
They arrived in breathless anticipation
Prepared to show their appreciation

Selecting two cats from the front of the crowd
The stars of the show shouted instructions aloud,
'Each grab an end of this rope if you will
Pull very tight and stand very still!'
Then placing upon it one ginger paw
Followed up by a further three more
Benny began to walk high in the air
Enchanting the watchers with his poise and dare

Next it was Kenny's turn to perform
With a flick of an ear and a nonchalant yawn
He stalked to the centre, spun around twice
Producing from nowhere five catnip mice
High they were juggled with feline grace
Faster and faster, gathering pace
His talent was rewarded with rapturous applause
From one hundred cats and two hundred paws

Suddenly the back door flew open wide
All the cats quickly ran to hide
Tabbies and moggies and Persians well-bred
Scattered under the bushes and behind the shed
From there they watched through almond-shaped eyes
As a human approached with plates piled high
A pungent waft of cod, place and prawn
Drifted up from the bowls and over the lawn

Whilst Kenny stretched out in glutinous glee
Benny scratched at a tiresome flea
Purring and padding at the human's feet
They waited eagerly for their tasty treat
With noses down and tails held high
They munched the feast with a contented sigh
No further thought given to their dreams and wishes
They had all they desired in two china dishes.

Miss Withakay

Ready

When I'm ready then I'll leave home and skip town
to live my potential dreams, when I am ready I'll set
up an unconventional place of legal tender and residence
and question my existence in a pondered, paced effort of
feel settled and happy or will I nomadly move on?

If I am ready does it mean I've found who I am and
understand my limitations? If I was ready would I be
financially stable and have the freedom to globetrot
travel and have many spiritual experiences in places
no one knew about?

If I was ready would I be married and conventionally
conform to a TV dinner partner who has a kitchen sink
existence with kids I never wanted and a wife I despise
who has no challenge of individuality or knows nothing
of decisive.

The pain of not knowing, yet knowingly intellectually that
my inertia would fade if I was ready, what a loser's game
to play, not being out of control of your future, 'cause my
path of adversity is trying to grip a hold of me saying,
'Get to know thyself.'

Then I'll be ready to philosophise my life, then I'll be
ready to feel comfy in my skin of flawed imperfections,
then I'll be ready to go the distance to venture out,
leaving behind my crutches, then I'll be ready to find
courage to do the things I fear.

But in the meantime I'll live life learning from mistakes
and attempting to grow up.
So when you're ready then maybe you'll stop punishing,
when you're ready, self-assuredness comes charging in
and when you're ready, clarity will aid you in personal growth.

Certain circumstances have to be gone through before
you give in and throw in the towel to come out the other side,
you won't even notice the changes, 'cause when you're ready
you'll get past your despondance and abolish all doubts
and wipe slate clean.

J A Carter

A Week In July 2005

3rd July
London staged a huge concert
To support all Africa's quest
To make their poverty history
Therefore putting the G8 to the test.

Famous stars gave up time for free
All ages joined in the applause
The whole world tuned in to the music
And the stars' desperate pleas for the cause.

Promises were agreed by world leaders
To cancel debts and so start anew
It probably won't yet make a difference
But it's a start, the least we can do.

6th July
Waiting for news from a far-off land
Everyone's nerves and breath held tight
Will London city stage the Games?
It surely now must be in sight.

Finally only two cities to choose from.
So quiet one could hear a pin drop
The final envelope opened,
London, the victory, leaving poor Paris in shock.

All of Britain was on a big high
As the celebrations and parties began
We could now plan the 2012 Olympics
As only the people of Great Britain can.

7th July
London was targeted by terrorists
Britain's celebrations brought to a halt
The silence not now in anticipation
But for the horror felt by us all.

How could they pick on the innocent?
Whatever or what be their cause
Killing or maiming is barbaric
So suicide bombers, expect no applause.

One thing these people never banked on
Was the spirit of everyone here,
They will never break our determination,
Londoners have stood many times against fear.

Violet Cook

Light Offering Virtuous Enchantment

In depth I see my way to you
It is tender power so true
A light in dappled haze makes clear dream
I walk in wood old, in light's gleam
Path to the heart of my desire
Is rich to live in light of fire
Drawing near to warmth of embrace
So calm I tread, this is no race
We clasp, my wish that grace will flow
In our hold, light be pure to grow
May smile play on face we see clear
In light's eye we held us so dear
A hand will touch, caress soft skin
The whole we are and live within
Let us walk a while in calm mind
See new view as we look to find
To not know is wish of heartbeat
With each pound we see us complete
True life grows strong, feel, give, believe
Through our wood we will slowly weave

We step one calm step hand in hand
Then stop to look at life's fine sand
We go slow and watch each grain drop
Time is now as we sow our crop
We flow as current in current
The way to give is abundant
This is of all, we look to seek
We will never know the true peak
As we look into our eyes bright
We will know sure there is true light
Come shine in us, with hope's plan wise
Acceptance will know real surprise
Foundation we'll dig and make strong
Through life hand in hand let's belong

Exquisite delight we seek bold
Our path, as us, we will unfold
Looking at us in hope so fair
We aim high and thus we dare
In courage our bliss will be found
Growing into light's fertile ground
Be our all, tranquil bliss shine
The way we walk is rich and fine

Our wood is fertile soil indeed
As we grow and dip deep then feed
Together in wood of deep song
New joys will soon to us belong
Butterflies will drink nectar sweet
Then shall fly to our wistful treat
In our heart's wood we slowly give
Now and in the future we'll live
Memory we know in our joy
We rerun bliss fine as fine ploy
For life is to see life in good
So birth in pain sees motherhood
This is the way, come new life start
In mother's pain we see fine art
As of life in us we reach out
For you and I we give, no doubt
We receive us then reflect free
As we walk through our wood and see
A new and ever-changing view
Deep in us our wood will renew
In slow steps fair we walk, deep thought
With us, is light the gift we sought?

Peter Ransom

I'm A Survivor

You don't understand my strength do you?
You think that I am weak
You think that I'm a pushover,
And will be told what to do
I understand that you are troubled
I know that you need help
But I am not the target here
I will not be shot down
You can't tell me what to do anymore
I'm going to stand my ground

You treat me like an infant
I was fourteen-years-old
You bullied me you selfish coward
You bullied my family too
I've picked myself up off the ground
I've brushed off all the dirt
I've straightened up my clothes and hair
And I'm looking you in the eyes

You lost any love I had for you
That went on Christmas Day
I've never had any pride in you,
In fact I am ashamed
You think you are the strongest one
The one we should all fear
But I'll be deadly honest
Look around and everyone you'll see
They pity you, you bully
No one is scared of you, you fool
We are the stronger ones now.

I'm a survivor: I made it through the years
So are my mother and my brother
And how we did it, I don't know
I was scared to put on make-up
I was scared to do my hair
I was weary when choosing clothes
I didn't want the volcano to erupt
You had me in a world of low self-esteem
My voice was never heard.

But look at me now Daddy, you can hear my voice
Look at what I'm wearing, do you think it's nice?
I'm not scared of you anymore, you should be scared of me
I'm stronger than you know, if you know me at all.

I'm stronger than you are
I can look you in your eyes
And I can say, 'I am a survivor,'
I thought you had killed my hope, my world,
I wouldn't give you the pleasure
Hold this message close to your heart,
And hold it there forever.

Layla Mallia (17)

The Optimist

Hungry, we go into the restaurant,
where a man with a large kitchen knife
sticking out of his chest appears at our table.

Removing it with a sigh he waves it in my face
and explains that this is an established business,
old, like Europe, waiting to be discovered
by someone who appreciates good cooking.

On the table a bunch of flowers wither.
The ceiling is low, as if we have not grown.
On the wall I see a picture animals understand.
Teeth and bone to record the application of blood.

Our waiter has been dead a thousand years.
Unconcerned he stores his images in a hotel vault.
Whispering in my ear he recommends the chaos rare.

Turning to me you see through my disguise.
I am hiding in a sea-green salad suit, making no sense
of it all, watering nearby plants, without a chest coughing.
Trying to calm me down you tell me I am being serious.

Out of empty wine glasses we drink in the new year.
Choosing history on the menu we pick at our meal,
masticating air, cleaning our white-hot empty plates,
asking for more, claiming death, our distraction complete.

With parted lips I watch food fall through holes
no longer trapped in your eyes' kitchen. A stranger
at the next table brings the largeness of imagination.

You offer me raw, red meat no longer spoiled by time.
Freshly killed, I taste inhuman reality, such is my love.
I am handsome without skin: you are pretty without eyes.

Slumped over the table, bits and pieces everywhere,
growing hungrier still, fresh screams make us invisible.
Throwing up our knives and forks, we cut the flesh of air,
removing outer layers with extraordinary patience to get inside.

Austin McCarron

Lady Lucia, The Garden Queen

There lived not so long ago in the tranquil suburbs of Harare
a lady whose house was graced with cut flowers
in shades of white, yellows and reds
blood roses hobnobbing with lofty gladioli
Cape marigolds with striped amaryllises
and carnations of the most delicate hues
I would enter its living room as in a sanctuary
before my visitors arrived
to relish those primeval fragrances
inhaling what to me was a whiff of Eden
for Eden or a parcel of it must look like the garden of Lady Lucia
how she would whisper to her flowers
still heavy with dew and inquire about their state
comment their appearance, with a slight frown
for she visited them as she arose
when the house was still lulled in dreams
as if they were guests of honour
to be doted on at every moment of the day
if she wasn't picking a withered petal here
pruning a bush of springbells there
or stroking her favourite dahlias
you could find her in the kitchen
concocting one of her Sephardic delicacies
baking almond cakes dipped in honey
filling jars with savoury biscuits and marzipan cookies
these occupied an entire shelf in the pantry
for there passed not a second day without a visit, whether the guest
just popped in to say a quick hello
or was invited to one of her fabled receptions
and though Lady Lucia never kept still
lavishing her hospitality on whoever
happened to cross her path at any given time
she always looked so lovely
a queen among her flowers

Albert Russo

Bluebell Girl

Walking in bluebell woods
Hand in hand
Pale blue dress
Laura Ashley flowers
Sunlight glowing in
Chestnut hair all rings and curls
Deep brown eyes
Standing serene
The sun on your face
Walking barefoot
My arm round your waist
You are my bluebell girl

On a coach, my head in a book
You came and sat beside me
At a party they play,
Dancing Queen
You laugh and pull me up to dance
Later in my car I pull you close
And we kiss for the first time
In your room a riot of sheep
Cover your bed
Morning sunshine
Your naked body next to mine
I've found my bluebell girl

You hate my job
You think I could do better
Perhaps I can
Another party, I kiss your friend
Your friend is very pretty
I can do better
We argue a lot
You start to cry
And return my ring
I'm relieved it's over
Now I am free
You were my bluebell girl

I see you with another man
I lose my rag, full of rage
I want to hurt you now
A busty blonde provides the way
She is everything you're not
And less, payback time
You hate her
She hates you
I'm happy
I can still cause you pain
I lied
You were never my bluebell girl

It's been so many years
Since I last saw you
I hear you're married now
A dog and 2 kids
I guess you have your cottage
With roses round the door
I ring you up
You sound the same
You say you're going grey
So am I
By the way did I ever tell you?
You'll always be my bluebell girl.

Andrew K Harvey

Guns Are Power's Seeds

Senses of powers are loves of kneeling.
Bondages to thrones are favours to needs.
Add a touch and tale all styles.
Gone glories are poor arrays.

Gone glories are a glossy of books.
Flake morals are glossed bloods.
Laser beams are on rivers of moons.
Last but not least are powers boosting.

Oppositions are airways to men's voices.
Last ditches are warrens that wide open.
Swear to play with no button down.
Vacuum controls are to power boxes.

Jack heads in boxes are not plums.
Gifts to darling are equal flux.
Love's a magnet to steal steels.
Powers are discs and rites to agree.

Live pockets are warrens as shields.
Prides are on tops and set in Aries.
Rocks and shock when waters flow.
Blows of money have many low downs.

Nobles are prixes and dears are loves.
Flex the maces are speeds of powers.
All human loves have machine codes.
Take your shares as weeds and molecules.

Birds' charms are live needles.
Men's guilds are lovers in-between.
Wicked candles are to certain degrees.
Accept morals as abandoned sheets.

I decline what I want to get.
Get me but do not finally take me.
Abased gods got the rule.
Junctions are where human crossing and able.

Blow by loves with frozen fleets.
To be aggressive is my advance sheets.
Within those advises are chats to knees.
With guns are those powers of bad seeds.

Cheung Shun Sang

In Tel Aviv

In Tel Aviv
Trees wither slowly
in the summer,
Elderly trees
Stuck in dry pits
Besieged by concrete
Severed from water.

In Tel Aviv
Trees are taken for granted
Exist as if by themselves
Burrowing desperately for water
In the dirt of the camel roads where they grew
In the junctions on the planes
that are now coated with asphalt.

In Tel Aviv
Trees that have turned brown
by the end of the summer
are cut down;
The Authority plants new ones
In the cavities, a variety without blooms
So that they don't mess up the pavements
When the blossoms fall.

In Tel Aviv
The workers will arrive in the cool night,
A Jew and a Palestinian,
Driving a small truck carrying a round
Water tank attached to a hose,
They will water the young plants twice a week
And collect their salary from the bank
Once a month.

I don't know how it is
In other cities of the land
But I've heard that in Argentine
There are no trees at all
Only huge grazing grounds
With cows
And they too are destined
For slaughter.

Liora Sara Bernstein

Colour Of Favourite

Mine is purple
Before that was blue
The one earlier was pink

What do the colours mean to you
I love red, it flows through me
It has passion and fire
And it does inspire me

I paint in red
Mix with yellow
It turns to orange
The colour of passion

The colours we see
Come in the seasons
Winter and summer
White and green
It is all beautiful to me

I love autumn
Neither hot nor cold
Neither wet nor dry
Longing to see the falling leaves
In the colour of passion

Now onto winter
When it's white and blue
But with the cold it brings
Some red noses too

When spring comes
The cold white gone
And the warmth of yellow appears
All quiet creatures
Back to live again

This is nature
So beautiful in all
A kaleidoscope of colour
There before my eyes
No wonder I feel so alive
No wonder I feel such pride

The Mother Earth nurtures us
In return we care for all
Not just human beings
But all living creatures
With her labour of love

The world is free
For all to enjoy
Man, woman, child and creature
This is how it should be
All underneath the beauty
Of a blue sky so free.

Mei Yuk Wong & Matthew Holloway

A Garden Scene

Halfway round our garden
one piece, is out of sight
of neighbours looking over
from houses left and right.
Bamboo, clematis, apple,
shield the rearward fence.
Vegetables grow well
behind the hedges dense.

A stump is all that's left
of a Bramley, gnarled and old,
the pond sprays out beneath it
with fishes red and gold.
Lie on the covered swing
to watch the scene spread out,
roses in the background,
a watering can with spout.

The sometime barbecue
is now a buzzing space,
with dragonflies and frogs
and honeybees in place.
Stonework adds to interest,
two herons, and a gnome
who's just lined up a Wellington
and thinks he'll take it home.

Over on the right side
beckons the arbour arch,
to glance at open fields
beyond a leafy larch.
Flowers edge green grasses
with colours of every hue.
The fountain merrily tinkles
in shining drops of dew.

Close by in the eaves
house martins nest their young,
twittering as the chaffinch
that spring has more than sprung.
And while the summer wiles
its way along the years,
God give us love and joy
with comfort for our fears.

A Audrey Agnew

The Children

I hear the voices again
Children's voices, subdued sometimes
Sometimes giggling
As if they were hiding from one another

Then calling to one another,
'Where are you?'
'I can't find you!'
'Come out wherever you are.'

The room was full of sunshine
Dust floating on the beams of light
As the wood in the old house
Settled in the warm sun.

I hear them running downstairs
And I step into the hall,
'Who are you?' I ask
And there is silence.

I can feel their presence
As though they watch me
Then I hear their voices again
Giggling and laughing together.

As they run back upstairs
Their footsteps echoing
In the quiet house
Then all is still again.

The past is ever with us
As is the future
And one is enfolded in the other
Time is but a measure.

The happiness of the boys
Enfolds me
Are they in a time warp
Or just shadows that come and go?

I will never know
Because I have to move on
To create my own impressions
Or shadows to leave behind.

Joan May Wills

Pleasure

The driving force of the senses
Which occupies body as vehicle
And mind as engine
Ignition usually sparked by a sight
Smell
Sound
Taste
Touch

The libido knows no limit
Each sense triggers the other
Body reacts as flush heat spreads across the skin
Shivering
Tingling
Prickles of sweat break the surface
Which is vibrating with an undercurrent
Of blood racing through the veins

Heart lurches forward into gear
A pneumatic
Pumping motor which revs the body into action

It has no bounds
Can drive for days
Or mere seconds
Depending on the fuel of the situation

Once begun
Causes sensations of excitement
In the psyche
Closed eyes
Smell and siphon the warm taste of ecstasy
Hear the ringing blood in the ears
Feel the thrumming of pleasure beneath the skin
Mind roaring
Energy flowing
Once fuelled
Pleasure can take us on a cruise
Comfortable and relaxing
Or
A wild intense joyride

Either way
Pleasure is only the driving force
The bounds of pleasure can only be pushed
Where the body wants to go

The responses are automatic
When the ignition is switched on.

Keep in control.

Emma-Jane Glenning

The Visit

Her sandy brown hair was all a mess,
Ice cream stains upon her dress.
Sitting on the curb of a no parking zone,
Appearing scared and all alone.

She sat silent, but tears filled her eyes,
My heart couldn't ignore her desperate cries.
I knelt down beside her, placed my hand on her arm,
I am here to help, I mean you no harm.

'Where is your mother?' I softly said,
She let out a sigh and lifted her head.
Her angelic voice quivered, 'I do not know,
She was just here a moment ago.

We came from the store where I dropped my ball,
I went to run after it, then I heard her call.
'Stay out of the street', so I stopped on the lawn,
When I turned back my mother was gone.'

I looked all around, there was no one in sight,
'We will find your mother, it'll be alright.
I will take you home, do you know the way?'
'I don't know my address,' she began to say.

'Can you describe your house, what colour is it?'
'It's yellow and white next to a big gravel pit.'
Thank goodness I knew the house she meant,
I took her by the hand and away we went.

Walking a short distance we could see her house,
This sad little girl became joyful and rouse.
She burst through the gate, her mum waiting there,
The woman only reacted with an empty stare.

She was totally oblivious to her daughter's return,
I approached the woman with great concern.
'Excuse me Ma'am, but are you OK?'
'I lost my daughter just yesterday.

She ran after a ball, but I yelled too late,
A reckless drunk driver decided her fate.
We bury her Thursday, then she let out a cry,
Why dear God did she have to die?'

I couldn't believe my very own ears,
Nor could I hold back my heartrending tears.
'You may not believe me, but I just have to say;
'I was visited by an angel today.'

I could never explain the why or how,
But I can assure you, she is with you now.
Together forever, never will you part,
As long as you keep her within your heart.'

Dawn Carol Drickman

Our Hearts And Minds

In a place some call 'the Emerald Isle',
for the past year or two has been home.
I'd never have guessed the effect it would have
on a man with a heart made of stone.

I knew not a thing of 'the troubles' out here,
but I learnt as my life trickled by.
The country so fine and its people so warm,
sure this 'war' it was surely a lie.

Of all of the folk that live here in this land,
just a few are enough to cause strife.
And to make themselves heard and force us to hear,
they've made themselves God and take life.

Some good people stood and said what they thought,
they raised up their doves made of card.
But those men without faces just mocked what they did,
and continued to fill the graveyards.

The political people from this side and that,
they spoke, promised, turned and condemned.
But the one thing they all could agree without doubt,
was this peace that's been broken must mend.

So here we are now and my son's turning ten,
and my daughter she's just become eight.
And it hurts in my heart to watch them grow up,
in this land that's torn up with such hate.

I watch them at night as they watch the TV,
and they hear about murders and all.
And it's now I realise that to give them a chance,
it's off we must be, job and all.

I don't want to leave this place I call Home
but I know what I do must be done.
I sit in my porch as the night wraps us up,
watching dreams fade and sink with the sun.

So we've packed up our bags and we're leaving at last,
this most beautiful country we love.
And I hope with my all that the peace does return,
and you'll no longer need your white doves.

My thanks for your time and may your God bless you all,
may the peace that you search for come through.
For understand this if you don't find it soon,
even God may give up and go too!

Peter Macdonald

A Return To Bruton

I'm off to Bruton town tomorrow,
    Down in Somerset,
I've long adored that gentle borough,
    I love it yet, you bet.

I'll hie me there in vibrant May,
    With toadflax on the walls,
When hawthorn and the lilac play
    Like fragrant waterfalls.

There's an ancient dovecote looking down,
    It eyes the slender valley,
Guards the tiny huddled town,
    Advises me to dally.

I'll saunter down to the happy place,
    Sweet bubble upon the Brue,
Gaze at the seats of scholarly grace,
    Of wealth and poverty too.

Appraise their architectural styles,
    Those rustic gothic stables,
The Tudor reformation piles
    With overhanging gables.

This peaceful pleasance, lacking frills,
    Was once a bustling place,
With racing waters driving mills
    That wove the cloth and lace.

Ruins of mills bespeak the skills
    Of men of olden days,
Of labouring men whose proud wills
    Must meet with my amaze.

In Sexey's chapel, craftsmen too,
    Deserve a round of acclaim,
For carving, oh, such stately pews
    In Charles' fatal reign.

Some of the high street dwellings hide
    A host of alleyways,
Where ghosties from the past abide,
    The folk of former days.

For down those passages toiled masses
    Of brewers, weavers, monks,
Laundry lasses, laden asses
    And tottering Saxon drunks.

They shut the alleys up at night,
    Bolted top and bottom,
And treated thieves and lovers alike,
    As like as not they shot 'em.

I'll take a peep down every alley,
    There's glaring light beyond,
And hear the rooftops in the valley
    Echo chaffinch song.

Then choose an alley and tootle down,
    Beside the balmy Brue,
Glittering in a green gown,
Gliding quietly through.

Terence Belford

A Story In Rhyme, A Friend In Need Is A Friend Indeed

I wandered home along that lonely lane
On a cold and wintry night
I felt so alone and unhappy
For nothing that day had gone right.

Rain that had been light was heavy now
There were tall trees that overhung
They gave no shelter from the rain
For all their leaves had gone.

A cottage dotted here and there
But not a soul in sight
Shut in the warmth against the cold
All shuttered up for the night.

As I travelled on to reach my home
I met an old black dog
His coat was so matted and mangy
His eyes were so terribly sad.

'Hello young fellow, you are all alone
You look as if no one cares
Come along home with me my friend
I've some dinner we two can share.'

He didn't need me asking him twice
He trotted along by my side
When we reached my home, he sat on the step
Till I said to him, 'Come on inside.'

I placed an old blanket in front of the fire
While he stood looking on
Then a drink of milk, and when I turned round
Curled up, and to sleep he had gone.

When he awoke I gave him a bath
Then brushed his coat till it shone
The two of us then shared my dinner
Till every last morsel had gone.

When I retired, I propped open the door
In case he decided not to stay
He wasn't really mine to keep
Though I'm sure he was only a stray.

In the early hours I crept down the stairs
Just to see if he was still there
Imagine my joy, as I pushed open the door
He was asleep on the old kitchen chair.

We have been together quite a few years
He guards my home every day
When I return from work each night
He meets me along the way.

I feel we were both two lonely souls
Who needed a very good friend
That chance meeting brought us together
With friendship that never ends.

Marjorie Garrett

Jack And Harry's Thoughts At Snap Time

When will this shift be over?
I'm ready to see light and no mistake,
Margaret will be just getting kids up.
It would be Heaven going home if I knew I wasn't coming back down
here again after what seems like a two minute break.

I hate that ruddy cage, I feel like a rat that's trapped,
In fact, that's just what I am like, a rat scuttling about under this earth,
Not looking for food, but coal.
God, what a hole!

'What's your mind on Jack? I've been talking to thi for last
ruddy five minutes,' Harry said.
I moved so fast I bumped my head on a pit prop. 'Oh Hell. Sorry Harry,
I were miles away just thinking about the light o' day.'
'The light of day Jack. It'll be about half past seven now,
sun just coming up. Folk'll be just wakening up
and listening to the birds.'

'Aye Harry, wife'll just be shouting at the kids
and not picking her words. I was thinking about the wife Harry,
you know, I don't tell her I love her anymore, not in so many words.
I'm too tired to bother after coming down here.
She's too tired to bother shedding a tear with seven kids,
Not soft like she used to be, she's all for the kids, no time for me.
God, I hate working down here, I hope my lads never do.
I don't want them to taste coal like me, Harry. What about you?'
'No, I don't want mine down a pit either,' Harry said.
'I just want 'em to use their ruddy heads and do better than me.
It's not hard though to do better than this,
Men must be mad for working down pits.'

'Still somebody has to Harry.
How can they make fires without any coal?'
'Aye Jack, and steelworks would shut and lots more places an' all.
There'd be no power for people in hospitals and they'd all die.
Old folk would freeze to death as well.
Our lass wouldn't be able to make me tea,
And the kids would be hungry and as mourngy as Hell.'

'You know when you come to think, we're important men me and thee,
they ought to award us an MBE.'

Well now we've finished our caviar and cocktails
(bread and dripping and water) let's get back to it Jack.'
'Aye Harry, see you on the way up to the top.'

Cindy Webster

The Strangest Thing

The strangest thing has happened to me
something so dark, so sinister, so blue.
To feel a life growing inside me, for it to die . . .
. . . my worst nightmare come true.

The emotional changes are drastic
from the centre of Heaven to the depths of Hell.
The roller coaster is fast and sickening
I can't believe the distance I fell.

How very quickly things can change
a harsh reminder of how fragile life can be.
Still, I don't understand and I'm so confused
can somebody please tell me, 'Why me?'

I feel so angry, so bitter, so annoyed
yet so hurt, so vulnerable and bruised.
Why did my life have to take such a sharp bend
a direction I certainly didn't choose?

How long can I go on feeling like this
so narrow-minded and self-indulgent?
I feel so guilty; there are worse things in the world
so what gives me the right to think I'm the *most* important?

As the days go by, I have to admit
that things do appear to be easing slightly.
I know it takes time, I'm accepting that now
just like I'm accepting the tremors I still get nightly.

I'm a strong person, I pride myself on that
and I will not allow this to keep me down.
Even as I write this I find my head lifting,
a smile breaking and I lose my bitter frown.

January is just around the corner
and I'm blessed to see in another year.
I place my future into the hands of God
and pray that I need not shed another tear.

I'm thankful for all that I have in life
and I'm sure that this experience will make me stronger.
With my wonderful husband and his continuous love
my positive spirit will go on for much longer.

Susan Macdougal

The Radcliffe Runner

What draws us to a marathon
Best of all, the London one?
    Britain's lines
    In lean times,
An electric hare 'is on'.

A greyhound, the female one,
Paula Radcliffe when having fun,
    Eating the miles
    Bobbing smiles,
Only, great runners, have done.

We love the speed of greyhounds,
The equivalent in human sounds,
    Oh glimpse Paula's side,
    In her beautiful stride,
God made her himself, in bounds!

It's true about African winners,
We seem to regard them as sinners,
    But Paula's strong gleams,
    In her eyes, it seems,
Tell us, of golden dinners.

Her nose while splitting the air,
Wind rustling her sandy hair,
    She's doing the thing,
    Under her wing,
Which everyone cares for, there!

Yes, she may, look frail!
It's what makes runners real,
    Her slippery frame,
    An urgent flame,
Best seen, on someone's tail.

With runners, any mistakes,
Can make a great body, to flakes!
    When breasting the tape,
    All eyes are a-gape,
Wondering, what's in, her laigs.

I have a Radcliffe cousin,
Who's only half a dozen,
    Of Paula's worth,
    In running girth,
But saucy in her loving.

Among the Roman gods,
Paula's statue is due in lots,
    P'raps Trafalgar Square,
    For people to stare,
With fat lions and other bods?

As birds when - migrating,
To us she's captivating,
    The brown of the land,
    Is desert sand,
When this camel, is on, the wing!

Don McIntyre

Death Of A Rainforest

The big knives are coming
We've not long to last,
Not long to stand here
They're coming so fast,
For a long time we've grown here
Since the threshold of time,
But now we are in fear
For our death bell doth chime.

The Creator, He planted
So long in the past,
A beautiful forest
To flourish and last,
A canopy so green
Spread under the sky,
Sustaining the Earth
Whilst soaring so high.

We nourish God's Earth,
We trees strong and tall,
Providing a home
For monkeys, parrots and all,
The people who live here
They fight for their land,
But others who come here
Just don't understand.

The big knives are coming
Oh! Now they are here!
High up in our branches
There is terror and fear!
The monkeys are fleeing
The parrots have flown!
For now they are seeing
The end of their home;
The people who lived here
Have moved far away

And now for we great ones
It's the end of our day,
No more can we nourish
The Earth and the sky,
For we are no more now
Our end has gone by.

Where once there was forest
There is brown earth and grass,
The days of our grandeur
Are now in the past;
Other people now live here,
They farm and they mine,
But they live in fear
Of an uncertain clime;
For the rains they still happen,
The storms and the flood
And their homes and their crops
Are swept away by the mud;
And now they lament us,
We trees strong and grand,
For it was God who lent us
To sustain the land.

Irene Hart

A Squaddie's Prayer

It seems so quiet and so calm
As I lay here on my bed
While all the horrors of this war
Spin around inside my head.

There are so many good men dying
Though I feel like a spectator
But I'm told that we must get rid
Of this evil, mad dictator.

A man who's got no respect
For any human life
And just intends to snuff it out
With a gun or bomb or knife.

His people whom he says he loves
He has them killed for fun
One day this man will have to pay
For the awful things he's done.

But it grieves me so just to think
Of all those who must die
From a bullet to the head
Or a bomb dropped from the sky.

Just a few short weeks ago
On a warm and sunny dawn
I sat watching from my window
As rabbits played upon the lawn.

Suddenly the phone rang
We had to go, and quick
I had trained for this very moment
But still nerves made me feel sick.

So now I'm in the desert
My rifle cocked and ready
I'm staring down the barrel
My hand is sure and steady.

I gently squeeze the trigger
And feel my weapon cough
And a hundred yards from where I lay
Someone's head's blown off.

Ordinary Iraqis, fright upon their faces
Look for safety in the smallest of places
In burnt-out cars, in holes in the ground
they crawl in to hide as the bombs fall around.

What manner of man is this Saddam Hussein?
Who inflicts on his people this terrible pain
In the name of Allah he tells them to die
In a hail of bullets or bombs from the sky.

With the might of the allies outside his front door
If he would give up he could stop this cruel war
But he forces his people upon fear of death
To fight on regardless until their last breath.

We hope that an end to the fighting is found
And that peace is restored to this once holy ground
Then people return to their land once again
Without the brutality of Saddam Hussein.

I'm missing my home, my children, my wife
All the things that I value the most in my life
I pray every day at the hour of dawn
That we'll all watch the rabbits at play on the lawn.

Kevin White

Herald Of Release

As I walked through an anarchic field of stone
I felt a wind of presence that softly tapped upon my shoulder
A whispering touch from the mountains thrown
Spoken in haste from stoic Earth's groan
Through growing desolation it did leap
Reaching me far colder

As I looked upon the looming trees of rock
The eaves of glass, the growing grass of slate
A visitor upon my door of consciousness began to knock
Rapping the frame of my thought, tapping mind's block
Through my spy-hole they did peep
Turning the handle of my fate

As I smelt the musty perfume of the street
The scents of the city assaulting my sense
This visitor of my mind I did turn and meet
Golden head down, eyes staring at stationary feet
Her intoxicating odours into my head did creep
Gripping like a concrete hindrance

I bent on one knee and looked up into her face
Turned my ear to hear her mumbling prose
But found nothing but a silent embrace
Arms hugging tightly in ephemeral grace
And leaving my heart to weep
She fled leaving nought but her scentful echoes

Lifting my eyes to see her leave I did see
Tears fall from her eyes and hit the ground
Breaking the slabs open that surrounded me
Cracking and grinding and setting all free
One solitary square of stone her tears did keep
The other fell into nothingness all around

Upon this rock on unsteady legs I did stand
Panicking and waiting to fall
Then the girl appeared and held out her hand
Whispering and pointing towards a bright island
The stone moved, towards the meadow we did sweep
Over the wracked city we did not stall

We softly landed on this patchwork of green
And she took off dancing along by the hill
Then she stopped and on tiptoes she did lean
Beckoning me over to stand by a stream
Trailing her fingers in the waters deep
Silently as I sat by her still

All of a sudden she halted, her head tilted
And spoke with an overwhelming peace:
'Your old life has become brown and wilted,
Your soul is no longer quilted
With a place where beauty can sleep
Never fear for I will put you at ease
Just remember me. Your herald of release'.

Tam Lamont

Oh Cornwall

Oh Cornwall, I am missing you,
I am not with you, so I'm feeling blue.
Your blue-green seas are calling me,
Of life's restraints, please set me free.

Polperro and Mousehole, your pull is strong,
Together again, please let it not be long.
The sea, sand and strong Atlantic waves,
Shells, coves and coastal caves.

Fishing boats and smugglers' taverns,
Overlooking wind-lashed, sand-blown caverns.
The magnetic pull of Holywell Bay,
To where I will return one fine day.

Moorland, heathland and standing stones,
Burial chambers with hidden ancient bones.
A land of plenty, a land of wonder,
Nowhere else I would rather wander.

Pasties, cider and Doom Bar bitter,
Clifftop walks to keep me fitter.
Oh Cornwall you are in my blood,
Be it rain, shine or even flood.

The wind in my hair, the sand in my eye,
Always I'm thinking of you, and you know why.
History and beauty combine into one,
In the south-west is where I belong.

I am dreaming of Tintagel, Padstow and Looe,
Oh Cornwall, I must come home to you.
I will move mountains to head your way,
This time around I intend to stay.

Sunrise and sunset over the Atlantic coast,
These are the scenes I love the most.
Watching the waves crash over the shore,
Lost amongst the sand dunes forever more.

Oh Cornwall, oh Cornwall to you I am lost,
I will reach you soon at whatever cost.
Devoting to you the rest of my life,
As I leave behind my current world of strife.

If you want to find me, head down the M5,
Fill up with fuel and drive, drive, drive.
Once in Cornwall, head for the sea,
Be still and listen and try thinking of me.

I will speak to you through the wind in the trees,
I will be watching over you from those blue-green seas.
I will be circling the land in the sweet Cornish skies,
Look to the heavens and stare into my eyes.

Kernow, I love you.

Nick Wright

Commuter

Crack of dawn - chorus bird is forlorn,
His sad absence I will mourn,
But what to keep him at his ease?
Any bees or trees?
No, just noisy metal boxes and HGVs.

Madly rushing, shushing,
A few fox-whistles, now I'm blushing,
Big delay, forever and a day -
Slow to make way, perhaps I will arrive to play!
Who cares anyway?

Traces of places in people's faces -
Anger and danger, irritation all embraces,
Warning to all in - don't look at their mourning,
The sadness and badness,
The self-induced madness.

Views from pews, slight peruse -
What's to see? Blocks of rocks, sometimes shocks!
But nothing really, over which to muse or even confuse,
Interestingly enough,
I'd rather look at my shoes.

Disembark, get ready to park -
And move along with the throng,
Shoving through, enormous queue,
You and you,
What monotony, nothing's new.

Swift advances, everyone dances with steely glances,
They all take chances,
Make a way out into the day,
Past a huddled chap in a cap who wants a chance
But doesn't win a single glance.

Out of sight, out of mind,
He's not usual, not one of *our* kind,
Avoid his glares, spring the stairs -
Get away and out of this hall,
Let's pretend he doesn't exist at all!

A light interlude in the day -
Work all hours for pay and pay
Until the hours, minutes, seconds are gone,
When the craving is here, right or wrong,
To once again become part of the throng.

Dead tired, in fact completely beat,
All that's wanted is a single seat,
But no, no . . . use your feet!
Aching body, much more rushing, shushing and even crushing,
Hot and steaming, tired of flushing.

Dissolve oneself in karma words,
Time out, to disregard and ignore all nerds - achtung!
The poor wee things, their brains are frying and in fact
They are dying - to be free,
Just like me.

Hooray, hooray, thank someone for that!
It felt like being drowned in a vat,
For a reason good I will search,
I'll think and I'll thank and rack my brain
As to why I should ever do *that* again!

Caroline Schuster-Cotterell

Auntie Maggie Tate

(Dedicated to the memory of Mrs Margaret Tate - 2001)

'It's only me from 43,' is what she used to say
when she called to see Gran and Grandad
for a cup of tea and a chat each day.

She'd pop her head around the door,
she had such an infectious smile,
whatever work she had to do she'd stay and chat a while.

She was loved by those who knew her,
yet I doubt we told her so,
known for her warm smile when you saw her,
Dad called her 'Our Mag' you know.

Once she threw a party to celebrate Bonfire Night,
she ate chewy toffee made by Maggie Entwistle -
it stuck her teeth together so tight.
It couldn't mask her bonnie smile,
nor could the cat who always gave her a fright!

Yes our Muttley loved her and went to her house so,
he'd leave a pongy deposit halfway up the stairs,
then out of her house he'd go!

Yet, Muttley was always welcome in Auntie Maggie's house,
he was a black cat that couldn't miaow
and rarely caught a mouse.

Auntie Maggie was warm and friendly
even to those she did not know,
yet she now has a new home in Heaven,
a new star in the sky has a special glow.

She has taken our love with her,
but happy memories she left behind,
what tribute could anyone pay her?
She was certainly unique and so kind.

As I sat in my garden and looked to the night sky,
I glanced a twinkle from a bright star,
guess Auntie Maggie's just passed by.

Goodnight and God bless you,
Auntie Maggie.

Michele Simone Fudge

Anchor Books – In Time & Motion

In The Year 3003

I watched, and I waited, but nobody came,
I trembled with fear, and man was to blame,
I watched, as the last plant did shrivel and die,
I watched the pollution darken the sky,
But nobody came.

I listened, as I waited, not a sound to be heard,
Not a rustle of grass, or the song of a bird,
In silence I strained for a distant sound,
Nothing was stirring; there is nothing around,
Only me.

There's no longer a fish to swim in the sea,
There's no longer a leaf to fall from the tree,
No longer crops seen on the ground,
The undergrowth's withered, where the snake was once found,
There's only me.

Gone the soft sunlight that shadowed the tree,
Gone the sweet breeze that once flowed free,
Gone is the spirit of man from the land of his birth,
Gone all life, from the revolving Earth,
But not me.

Who was it that said the world needs cheaper fuel,
More nuclear stations? Yes man, you fool.
Who was it that buried radioactive waste in the ground?
Who was it that said it was safe? Yes, safe and sound.
It was not me.

Yes, the wealthy and powerful have fled from your Earth,
Yes, have abandoned their planet for another birth,
Yes, no one listened in the year two thousand and one,
Years after the time, leaking radiation began,
No one listened but me.

Now with a spirit that's weak, and a soul in disgrace,
I see human destruction face to face,
As I look through the darkness, there is something I see,
The empty conscience of the silent me,
Still nobody came.

Laura Clarke

Heigh-Ho For The Open Road!

Gone are the joys of motoring,
When driving, one felt free;
A country run, a camping trip,
A day out to the sea;
No traffic jams - nothing felt finer,
Than an outing in our Morris Minor.

And now it seems we all have dreams
Of a bigger car than yours,
Forget the fumes - that global thing -
We need our four by fours
With double crash bars at each end
To make the car complete,
To fend off all those herds of cows
That clutter up our streets.

And children, in the playground, say
Not to appear a fool,
'Our car's a Shogun, which Mum needs
To drive us both to school.
The walk from home is half a mile -
For us it's far too far.'
Much better to sit muffled up,
Strapped into Mum's new car.
We asked the girl that if a walk
As exercise would suit her?
'Exercise - yes - we all have that,
Two hours on the computer.'

Visiting Japan I quickly found
Their driving rules go far.
If you don't have an off-road park
You're not allowed a car.
Can you imagine in UK
If this became a rule?
No cluttered roads, and clean, fresh air
And kids that walked to school.

Our country's 'tops' in many things,
In transport, it is not.
One wonders often as I do,
If Whitehall's lost the plot!
Perhaps solutions they'd derive
If grid-locked on the M25!

D H Tanton

The Story Of Life

The bare-branched tree stands
Stark against the wintry sky;
Its rime-covered skeleton
Reaches out up high
As if in humble supplication
To our Heavenly Father
For sustenance and succour
Throughout the bitter weather.

Spring comes, the tree survives,
For God's goodness is profound.
Upon its limbs new buds appear;
Plants cover sun-starved ground.
Buds flourish and deck the tree
In a gown of glorious green,
Within whose pleats and ruffles
Busy nesting birds are seen.

As the year progresses
Foliage gets more profuse,
And beneath its branches
Welcome shade's put to use
By people and animals alike
In these long halcyon days,
And among its twisting roots
All manner of wildlife plays.

Autumn comes, the season when
The tree must change her gown
To one of yellow, flame-red,
Orange or biscuit brown;
She's looking her most beautiful
At this point in time;
Her swansong, for too soon
She'll be stripped by frost and rime.

And so the year's gone by;
We're back to winter drear
When all appears dead, but
Dear friends, have no fear;
This same tree standing stark
Against the wintry sky
Will burst forth again to glorious life
In the sweet by and by.

Marlene Allen

Whatever/Whoever

It matters not to me who you are,
you will never take my God from me.
You may use words - politically incorrect,
you may take my Bible book from me,
but, I am what I am at God's volition,
and no one, from Pope to politician
can take who, or what, I am from me.

I had a parent who taught to me
that I am what I was meant to be,
and that, if I had not been taught about God,
no matter what, I would have known about God,
and, this same parent also told to me
that I must never let a church break my heart,
because, there is God, and establishment,
and I must learn to tell them apart.

I had a grandparent whom I never met,
but, the same parent told me that I must never forget
that religion and politics were not allowed in his home,
it was his Bible, his volume, his tome.
All who argued the fact were shown the door.
It would be his way for evermore.

He died too young to ever see,
that as Irish Catholic as he could be,
and, as Scottish Protestant as was his wife,
my loving grandma, he was right about life.

If he could return, he would be amazed
at the way his future family fazed.
We are so mixed, yet, we love one another,
be we Protestant, Jewish or RC,
we love God and each other, as it should be.

So Grandpa, thank you, no matter who they be,
they will not take my God from me.
My Bible is God, He is in my heart,
and, no intolerance will ever part
me from my God, but, will make me see
what you tried to teach your family.

We are born, we live, we die, we lie beneath stone cairns,
but, as we say in Scotland we are a 'Jock Tamsin's bairns',
and, if we love Him, no matter what His name,
we should only do good, for we are all the same,
no matter who, or what you are,
you cannot take my God from me.

A Bible is not a book, you see,
it is faith, His word, engraved
in my soul eternally,
and, in His name, we do no ill,
and, in His name we do not kill.

We must all face Him one day,
God of mine, I hope and pray
You love me for who and what I be,
I love You for who or what You be!

Mhairi Jarvis

Gloria The Crab

Bobbing alone on the crest of a wave
    In a discarded cigarette packet
Was a hermit crab called Gloria
    In a wonderful silver shell jacket.

She had left the harbour at quarter to three
    As the packet was tossed from the wall
It floated down gently beside her
    As its owner was taking a phone call.

Not wanting to be caught by a fisherman's hook
    She scrambled aboard as it passed
Just out of the flight path of a seagull
    As it dived in the briny so fast.

Her vessel turned left as it went out the gates
    She held on tight with a claw
Waved politely with one of the others
    At a haddock who smiled with huge jaws.

Now Gloria had lived a sheltered life
    Tucked down by an anchor chain
Near the outfall sewage pipe
    She never had cause to complain.

Plenty of barnacles and crustaceans
    The occasional well-formed shrimp
One thing for sure she was never hungry
    Never came over all limp.

So now finding herself out on the ocean
    Was becoming a scary affair
As the packet was getting a bit soggy
    The silver paper was beginning to tear.

Now wishing she'd taken her chance with the gull
    And the fisherman's hook
She peered over the side and into the waves
    Her selection of claws just shook.

Beginning to cry as evening approached
    She felt that her life was done
When out of the blue a voice she heard,
    'Gloria what have you done?'

She opened her eyes and there close beside
    Was a huge jolly turtle called Jack
He held out a fat flipper saying, 'I'm not a kipper
    Gloria get onto my back.'

She clambered aboard feeling rather ashamed
    As her packet sunk out of sight
The moral being you don't take to the sea
    In a vessel that's really not right.

Jennifer Steddy

The Battle Of Copenhagen

A damned cold wind it was and raw
When Nelson crossed the sea,
To fight the Danes in naval war
And gain supremacy.

He waited long off Elsinore
For orders from Hyde Parker;
The doughty admiral in command
Liked not the coming slaughter.
And a damned cold wind it blew and raw
With Nelson's ship confined offshore.

At last the message came to sail
And head for Copenhagen,
Nelson knew he could not fail,
His gunnery would save him.
The damned cold wind it blew and was raw
When Nelson's ships passed Elsinore.

With frigates, sloops, and twelve gun brigs
He braced himself for action,
The wind had veered the night before,
Dispelling need for caution,

His band of brothers on the deck
Had formed a ring of courage,
With gallant Nelson in their midst
They stood to face the barrage;
The gunsmoke billowed round the mast
But gunners all withstood the blast.

The signal came to disengage
And leave the grisly battle,
The sea was strewn with blood of men
Who died like slaughtered cattle.
A damned cold wind it was and raw
As this sad flotsam washed ashore.

Hyde Parker knew the odds were grim
And called for a withdrawal,
But Nelson the protagonist
Preferred a free for all.
The wind, inclined to moderate,
Condemned the Danes and sealed their fate.

Then Nelson raised his telescope
In sightless recognition,
'I see no signal, lads!' he cried,
And won the day for Britain.
And the damned cold wind it blew and was raw,
As they sailed back home, past Elsinore,
And pondered why they'd gone to war.

Sylvia Horder

A Part Of Me Is Missing

Part one

A part of me is missing now
I have surely been torn in two
I can't imagine how you're feeling
Or what you're going through
I can't live with this imbalance
Or hide behind the pressure
I know you've been gone a while now
My god, it seems for ever
I am distanced from the sense of purpose
Which once meant so much
A mother's instinct, isolated
I need to see you, smell you, touch
Well I'm getting tired of all this now
And I can hardly stay awake
My tension is taking control of me
I'm stretched further than I can take
My inner voice is telling me
I must set out with a firm intention
But I can't see a change
When I'm going in the wrong direction
I've been backed into a corner
A strange world where I don't want to be
There's just so much I don't understand
And I'm finding it hard to breathe
I wish I knew where you were
But I'm not allowed to know
Maybe just a glimpse of you
Why can't they please come home?
I'm told to face this challenge
But I'm under too much pressure
Instincts are so demanding
Please give me back their pleasure
I'm a stereo with no volume control
No one seems to hear me
None of this makes any sense
A way forward is impossible to see
I've got to get out this hell

My intuition urges me on
But they juggle with my emotions
Where have all these rules come from?
The pointless advice is endless
It seems that no one cares
My children are suffering
It's all so damned unfair.

Lucy Campbell

Praise The God Of All Creation

(Can be sung to the hymn tune from Beethoven's 9th Symphony Ode To Joy)

Praise the God of glowing colours
Pastels, tints and shining hues.
Praise the God of all creation
Praise in purples, greens and blues.
Praise the God of shining jewels
Sparkling, glistening in the light.
Praise the God of all creation
Praise in rubies, zircons bright.

Praise the God of hedge and field
Food and beauty for our need.
Praise the God of all creation
Praise in plant and flower and seed.
Praise the God of vibrant flowers
Daisies, roses, hollyhocks.
Praise the God of all creation
Praise in pinks, forget-me-nots.

Praise the God of clothes and fabrics
Clothing us with warmth and skill.
Praise the God of all creation
Praise in denim, lace and twill.
Praise the God of paints and canvas
Landscape, portrait, still life scenes.
Praise the God of all creation
Praise in jade and ocean green.

Praise the God of stained glass windows
Telling stories to inspire.
Praise the God of all creation
Praise in glass and lead and wire.
Praise the God of faithful rainbow
Transient promise paints our sky.
Praise the God of all creation
Praise in rain and cloud on high.

Praise the God of mystic meaning
Holy Spirit, purple peace.
Praise the God of all creation
Praise in liturgy's increase.
Praise the God of my creation
One who formed and colours me.
Praise the God of all creation
Set in brilliant harmony.

Heather Marion Lee

Walking Past My Old School

If I could only float in a boat of my alright-ness
On a sea of my alone-ness
But still I tread the pavements muddied with chocolate
See scenes and schemes of laces and lunchboxes
Of coats as cloaks and shoes scuffed on the gravel
The coloured code of sweetie wrappers and sticky fingers
And banks of eyes following me left and right

I still see trees for climbing, walls as tightropes
The unbelievable freedom of a clear road ahead
When they talk to me I'm alive
They're twittering like birds
Like spring tapping on the shoulder of winter
I've waited too long to hold my baby in my arms
It means too much to ever happen

My children talk to me, just as yours do
I see you walking, your babies orbiting you
Our eyes don't meet though I look at you
You're carrying keys and plimsolls and paintings of people
You herd them and scold them, ride their banter like a centurion
And I imagine that I am you
That I don't have to create my children in my head
That I will cook with them and dance with them
Read them stories at night and hold them when they are afraid
Hug their little shoulders, breathe in their skin, their hair
They're there

The trees don't want to turn to autumn
Life rushes past me, time ticks in pain
And I stay empty, weary
Worry that my soul is as dry as the desert
That there is a part of me that will forever be unused
Like a doll in her box, pristine, collectable
That I will never flex my motherhood muscle
That I'll be the thinnest, richest, angriest person in the world
And nobody will know how I died inside
Walking past my old school

Debbie Tyler

The Bewick's Swans

There is a chill across the tundra wastes,
the summer ends, so nature states;
swans must look for pastures new,
just like other migrants do;
the Bewicks know it's time to go;
their heart and conscience tell them so,
friends and families of past years
leave their home and shed no tears.

They cross ocean, sea and land,
for reasons only they do understand;
heading south and seldom seen,
to Vermuydens' washes with pastures green;
in tight formation with leaders bold,
this ancient journey, a course they hold;
they chatter as they fly this course,
and forget the past with no remorse.

In the washes, courtship occurs,
and symphonies of birds are heard;
that honking sound, it is their call,
heard from Salters Lode to Fortrey's Hall;
they feed upon the fields of beet,
and when that is gone they graze the wheat.
Fen farmers are their friends of old,
and always have been, so we are told.

Many birds come and winter here,
mostly from the northern hemisphere;
whoopers, geese and ducks and wigeon
adorn the fenland skies alongside pigeon;
a spring day will come, that is for sure,
a sign to leave the fens once more;
that honking sound from in the sky,
does bode farewell, that cry.

Rex Sly

If

(Inspired by 'If' by Rudyard Kipling)

If you can think on your feet in a hurry,
and not react when fingers of blame point at you,
then without any qualms, pass the buck using charm,
then this advice is just perfect for you.

If you can trust yourself when all others doubt you,
and with guile turn their doubt into trust,
if you can hide your impatience while waiting,
wearing the countenance of the honest and just.

If on being lied about, you can lie even better,
or being hated merely note vengeance due,
and can live by the simplest doctrine,
'do unto them before they do to you'.

If you can keep your real face hidden,
giving nothing away with your eyes,
and always look at your very best
and appear wiser than those you despise.

If you can live out your dream like a master,
if you can out-think and out-scheme in the name of the game,
if you'll do anything to triumph or avert a disaster,
making sure that your enemies get blamed.

If you can smile to hear that the 'truths' you have spoken
are accepted as gospel by gullible fools
and never let the things that you value get broken,
even if that means bending or changing the rules.

If you can ignore the injustice
of poor healthcare, policing and schools,
if you can convince the masses,
that the media are liars and fools.

If you can force your heart and nerve and sinew
to follow your dream ever upward and on
and ignore those that fall by the wayside
even long after your own goal is won.

If you can convince the crowds that you're with them
and with kings use the very same touch,
and when in due time, friend or foe cannot hurt you,
because none of them really matter that much.

If you can fill every unforgiving minute
with sixty seconds worth of scheming well done,
yours will be the Earth and everything that's in it,
and what is more; you'll be a politician my son!

Peter Clay

A Wee Lad's Introduction To Church

When a wee child, my Auntie May decided I'd had too much play
  And on a fine bright Sabbath day she took me to her church to pray.
Taking books off a pile she pulled and tugged me down an aisle,
  Pausing to bestow a smile on others sitting there in style.
Pushed into a pew, despite my plea, with a column in front I
                                   couldn't see,
  I thought, *it's just as well maybe - if I can't see them they can't*
                                   see me.

My aunt had rituals to reveal - 'Before you sit you have to kneel.'
  So - with downturned toe and upturned heel I wriggled at a
                                  wobbly keel.
On a well-worn pad my knees sojourned and I heard the prayers
                            my aunt had learned.
  But feeling somewhat unconcerned my head I slowly backward
                                  turned.

A lad behind had a sullen pout (a little creep I had no doubt),
  He stared as I poked my tongue out - my aunt gave out a
                                stifled shout,
'You naughty boy!' She clipped my ear, a quiet, 'Sorry,' to the rear.
  'He's not my son you know, my dear, I'll tell his parents never fear.'
Then, down the aisle in gay attire, 'Get on your feet - here comes
                                the choir.'
  Some sang low and some sang higher - smiling, beaming, to inspire.
'Ah! here's the vicar.' 'What a shock - a bloke dressed in a long
                              white frock.'
  'What's he doing in the dock?' 'He's going to address his flock.'
I looked around - where's the sheep? Then I saw the little creep.
  His tongue this time my way did peep - I nudged my aunt,
                                revenge to reap.
'Keep quiet and sing the hymn,' she muttered. 'Can't do both at
                            once,' I uttered.
  My hymn book fell from the shelf - all cluttered, without the words
                          I stammered and stuttered.
Then - off again - sit, stand and kneel - this bobbing lark had
                              lost appeal,
  I began to feel like a dog must feel when by his master is called
                                to heel.
'Upon your feet to say the Creed - a very special prayer indeed.'
  If so special why the need to babble through it at this speed?

Seemed to me to be absurd, for, if we all should feel quite stirred
　And meaning every single word - why gabble at the pace I heard?
Now! What's this here - out of the blue, from hand to hand along
　　　　　　　　　　　　　　　　　　the pew?
　A plate was passing from and to - I wasn't sure what was to do.
There seemed to be some money there - I hope the plate would
　　　　　　　　　　　　　　　　　not be bare
　And that they'd hand me out my share - otherwise it seemed unfair.
Ah! Here it comes - I gave a grin and made for a coin inclined to spin
　When a voice from behind cried, 'That's a sin - you don't take it
　　　　　　　　　　　　　　　out, you put it in.'
The last hymn was sung and we heard the grace and all departed
　　　　　　　　　　　　　　　at shuffling pace,
　The vicar shook hands and admired my face - quite unaware of
　　　　　　　　　　　　　　my shame and disgrace.
Outside once more my aunt cried, 'Look here - you pray for
　　　　　　　　　　　forgiveness - have I made that clear?'
　Promise me this and I won't tell your dad, 'With my halo a-shining,
　　　　　　　　　　　　　　'I'll be a good lad.'
So skipping along free from all fear - sins all forgiven and now in
　　　　　　　　　　　　　　the clear
　To be good, understood, forever I'd try - but first let me give that
　　　　　　　　　　　　　creep a black eye.

*Note: I'd like to add - the lad is fictitious - unlike him - I'm far from
vicious.*

Eric E Webb

What Is Happiness?

I met a man without any arms, a pleasant man to meet,
When I mentioned his affliction he said, 'I have two feet.'
I can walk and talk and see my friends in village or in town,
I can appreciate God's world around me so there's no need for
                                                    you to frown.'
I met a lady with no legs who used a wheelchair to get around,
She told me she was lucky as many folk were totally housebound.
'Don't waste your time on pitying me,' she said, 'you drive me up
                                                    the wall,
There are many people in this world who can't get around at all.'
I met a man who could not hear, he had to read people's lips,
He was a very clever man and passed on several good tips.
'Don't you worry about my problems, just try to be sincere,
Because I can see my children's faces and cuddle them with care.'
I met a lady who is blind and as I took hold of her hand,
I tried to be helpful to her, I could not understand
That she could be so happy, but this she said to me,
'I can hold a conversation, hear the birds and tunes sound good
                                                    to me.'
I met a man who could not speak, my words stuck in my throat,
But he made me understand his case by passing me a note,
'I can hear and see and walk around and can use either hand,
That is why I am happy, don't you really understand?'
I met a child who was handicapped, who greeted me with a smile,
A happier child you would never meet if you travelled many a mile,
There was no need to feel sad as this child really enjoyed life,
Even filled with pain and full of trouble and strife.
I met a couple who had everything, big house and motor car,
They always took their holidays in warm countries near or far,
Their bank balance was so designed its value never came down,
But whenever you should meet them they always wore a frown.
So weigh up all the pros and cons before sympathy you give,
Remember happiness is a state of mind and not how well you live,
So if you see people suffering, give them help in moderation,
They do not need your sympathy but they do need consideration.

Help the deaf, the blind, the lame, whenever chances come your way,
Don't let time for helping the afflicted wait till another day,
Be helpful, cheerful, do good deeds and cheer up those who
                                                    are bored,
Then you will find true happiness will be your just reward.

Stan Gilbert

Words

Words form lines and columns, march like an army in
                                     numbered legion,
They are influenced by slang and mannerism, unique to
                                     geographic region.
Each county boasts its own derivation, expressing love, hate,
                                     hope and doubt,
The less demonstrative use eyes and lips, others wave their
                                     arms about.

They inspire, inform, educate, delight, encourage, charm, condemn
                                     or curse,
Are collected in condensed format in dictionary, reference book
                                     or verse.
Discover them in magazines, road signs, shops, schools, workplace,
                                     legal jargon,
Pubs, newspapers, space and time capsules, cars, sales, 'Fancy
                                     a bargain?'

Words pour out from television, radio set, music, cassette and internet,
Travel long distance with passengers in coach, train, ship and
                                     jumbo jet.
Journey through fax machines and telephones in varied vocabulary,
In blunt or dulcet tones, 'Emergency! Fire, ambulance
                                     or constabulary?'
They are unique to people, who compose, read and speak,
Exceptions to this rule are sometimes found in creatures with a beak.
Some originate in ancient times, were scratched on papyrus,
While others are erased or rearranged, struck down with
                                     computer virus.

Instruments utilised include biro, crayon, pencil, standard or propelling,
In modern mode, inkjet or laser printer cover sports
And political, critical storytelling,
The pen is mightier than the sword,
Can destroy with cutting remark or give thanks,
May articulate gently or fire pointed remarks and loaded questions
                                     from think tanks.

Words help to make the world go round, italics, bold, large print
or Braille,
Sometimes communication breaks down, but they usually tell a
good tale.
Essay, essay, essay, looking for Miss or Mister Write,
Check for letters following their name to prove they are qualified
and erudite.

Always study the small print, never take everything as read,
Learn a European language, display your linguistic street cred.
Encourage comprehension diction, sculptured, crafted, refined
As opposed to crude and uncouth outpouring of the four letter kind.
Aim for capital behaviour, don't step out of line or serve a sentence,
Being a captor is best left out the chapter and may lead to repentance.
Allow some space for a medicinal laugh inside a paragraph,
Employ a page to furnish a volume of wine in a handsome carafe.

Words are immensely versatile, take synonym, delineate,
onomatopoeic, phonetic,
Applied in dictation, intonation are objective, reflective, past,
present or prophetic.
From 'gaga goo goo', 'Baba', 'Mama', 'Dada', first lessons we
receive from birth,
We derive pleasure from the application and appreciation
of *Wordsworth*.

Dennis Overton

A Mother's Wish

A friendly face looked up at me
And with a deep breath said,
'Come my dear, sit right down
Beside me on my bed.

The love you all had for me
Will live on from day to day,
In your hearts and in your minds
I would like to say,

Caring for you all, to me
Wasn't such a chore
But alas time had come,
There was no quick cure.

Remember me as your wonderful mother,
Look after Dad, sisters and brothers.
I will look down on you wherever you go
And be beside you - you'll feel the glow.

I am in a picturesque place,
Pain free now, just filled with grace,
I've met family and friends I haven't seen for a while,
You can see them too just give a smile.

Tell the grandchildren I'm with them
Every step of their way,
Look after them as I did you
Until we meet again some day.

So now peacefully time has come
For me to close my eyes,
Don't shed a tear, please be strong,
No one ever dies.

They live on as long as you want,
There is no time to spare,
God bless everyone I knew
And all those that really cared.'

Jan Nice

VE Night

Red, white and blue the ribbons were
Which we wore with such great pride.
Full of joy, and delight on every face,
Our happiness we couldn't hide.

VE Night meant 'Victory' here
In Mundesley-on-Sea,
We sang, we clapped, we jumped with joy,
Our hearts were filled with glee.

Millie Gaze was playing the piano loud
As we danced around the Square,
The revelry went on late into the night,
All the village was there.

In fun, Vivienne's mum was in a deep-bottomed pram,
Dressed as a baby small
With a dummy, bottle and bonnet too,
Looking quite cute, I recall.

Brothers and dads were coming home,
It cheered the hearts of each girl and boy,
So happy we were we almost burst -
O what a night of joy!

Down at the Watch House on the Sea Front
Mr Strong, Uncle Reg, Shirley, Mary and Moll were there,
All were elated and having a sing,
Even a large tipple of beer!

A bonfire was lit on the car park nearby
To celebrate the peace,
Soldiers marched up the Sea Front road,
Soon would be their day of release.

The War was over, we were free,
Our folks would all come home,
Peace was here to stay for aye,
Victory had been won!

Mollie D Earl

A Widow's Only Son (Captain Ginger) 1917

Night, and with it came not the well-earned rest of toiling day
But work, stern and grim, an act in the drama, a battle was about
to begin

No moon rose in the heaven's above, no gentle murmurings
Like the cooing of a dove
For a storm was rampant o'er the plain like a thousand friends
plunged in pain

Highly-strung and quivering was each man with excitement,
Like hounds on a leash
Eager to make the foeman fly, eager to do and win or die
Just before dawn the order came round, 'Stand to,' and without
a sound

We crept to the tips of the ridge just in front
And a stray bullet's billet was marked with a grunt

In sectional rushes, 'Proceed from the right,'
The next order came and we were into the fight
Of good British stuff, not one was afraid
They fought with great coolness, as if on parade

All officers wounded, we'd better retire
Not us, t'would be foolish in this devilish fire
'Follow me,' a sergeant cried to the men
An act that well-earned him the DCM

'Cease the rushes and form a line
But blaze away at 'em all the time
Then wait for my signal, I'll give you a shout
Then, altogether, we'll rout 'em out'

'Charge,' the cry came as from a clarion clear
And we swarmed o'er the hill, unconscious of fear
Each Tommy was fighting, and fighting his best
Whilst hoping and trusting in God for the rest

The blow was struck, the field was ours
And as I fell, by a patch of flowers
I saw them bring my comrades in
On their faces, smiles, or death's queer grin

It was a terrible battle up Sheria way
And God forbid that I may say
See that place, where weary and worn
My comrades lay sleeping, killed that Sunday morn

'Twas a great day for our division
They earned undying fame
They bore the brunt of the whole attack
And it was part of the civilised game (war).

Frank Senior

Grandpa

My grandpa was a 'Teddy boy'
(He showed me the photos)
The 3 inch quiff at the front of his hair
Was his pride and joy, as well as
The crepes and drapes he used to wear.

He always says, 'those were the days'
(He showed me his shoes)
And he rubs his hands with glee
'We would all dress up on a Friday night
And go out on the town for a spree.'

He often wore a shoelace tie
(He showed me a blue one)
With a white shirt and blue suit
He says all the girls fancied him
Because he looked so cute.

He still has all his records
(He showed me every one)
And he plays them once in a while
They sound so old and scratchy
But they make my grandpa smile.

He used to sing like Elvis
(He showed me the words)
But his voice was never strong
We bought him a karaoke machine
And he likes to sing along.

He danced at my mum and dad's wedding
(He showed me the video)
His crepe-soled shoes still fit
He said he's a jiving expert
And he is still very good at it.

He talks a lot of the old days
(He showed me some scrapbooks)
It all seems a lot of fun
Now he lives on his own with his memories
They are precious, every one!

Sally Hall

The Mouse

His pinpoint eyes are pink and bright,
His coat is white as milk.
His tail is long and flexible
And feels like corded silk.

Sometimes a lightning flash will streak
Across my polished floor.
At other times he's jet-propelled
Or like a dynamo.

He's not the type to take his time -
He's always in a hurry!
We're all agreed he's hooked on speed;
His favourite word is 'scurry'.

He'll forage for some crispy crumbs
To have a tasty crunch,
And if he sees a piece of cheese,
He'll have a gourmet lunch.

If I find a yellow label
Shredded like confetti,
I'll know he's in my kitchen bin
Eating Heinz spaghetti.

He's very quiet as a rule,
But now and then he squeaks.
He's trying to communicate
For that is how he speaks.

He's clean and cute and comical
And such a clever chap.
He won't be caught in pussy's claws,
Nor run into a trap.

He's such a friendly fellow,
This cheeky little mouse.
I'll welcome him outside my door -
But never in my house!

Celia Thomas

Bang

We stand proud and tall in immaculate line
And receive the orders by which we're impressed,
To wage war on regimes that they malign,
Our cause is so worthy we're sure to be blessed.
We march off to war as the cheering applause,
Soundtracks in our heads while we prepare to die,
Trumped up with fervour our lionheart roars,
So trusting of betters we never ask why.

The battle commences, too easy by half
To wipe out those Evils who'd caused you such dread,
Was that who you're scared of? Don't make me laugh,
You're sure you're not thinking of others instead?
Our laughter's a refuge from guilt that we feel,
When facing the carnage we've wrought on the brave,
People we've killed in this war; it's surreal,
We massacred those we intended to save.

'The price is worth paying,' they said as we left,
'To liberate a nation that's under the yoke.'
They haven't a clue, our leader's bereft
Of ideas on clearing the fire and smoke.
What price compensates for the wail of a child
Who stands among debris of innocence killed?
Grey eyes stare blankly at corpses high piled,
The gardens she played in are a killing field.

The price that's demanded is seen in the eyes
Of murderous crowd who surround me with hate,
Abandoned by allies and caught by surprise,
I'm left to their mercies, that control my fate.
My crusade is ending before it's begun,
A rifle is pointing sure straight at my head,
Our leaders can't number these mantraps they've spun,
So shirk in their duties to those they have led.

A soldier's a stoic from day he accepts,
Commission and rifle, he's ready to die,
Small part in fortune of other's precepts,
But tragic when knowing he dies for a lie.

Bang!

James Melrose

Tattered Teddy

The attic room was cold and empty,
It was very dark and dusty,
In one corner lying there was a tattered teddy bear
Left by the children who didn't want him any more,
So poor Teddy lay there thinking what to do,
I'll go on an adventure to far off sunny lands,
Take my bucket and my spade and build castles on the sands.

I want to shake hands with the monkeys,
Ride on an elephant's back,
Play chase with lions and tigers
And watch a crocodile smile,
I will climb the highest mountain
And put a flag on top,
Then off to Australia to see the kangaroos hop,
There are many things I want to do,
If you were me, would you?

As Teddy lay there dreaming
The attic door flew wide,
A little girl called Polly came running inside.
Polly saw poor Teddy lying all alone,
She picked him up and told him, 'This is your new home.'
The hole in his tummy was mended,
His fur was given a wash,
A new glass eye and a red bow tie,
How handsome Teddy was.

But what about your adventures Teddy
And all you wanted to do?
We rode on a rocket right up to the sky and polished the sparkling stars,
We went to the woods and met Robin Hood,
Climbed the tall trees to the top,
Polly and me sailed away on the sea,
We came home at half past three,
Just in time for tea.

Mary Neill

The Squirrel In Thomas' Grandma's Garden

What has happened to the oak tree?
Why is it missing today?
It's going to be hard to jump
From this tree to the next
Without the oak to help me on my way.
I'm very upset, and truly vexed,
I'd like to cry, but I must try
To make an enormous leap,
So here goes -
Jump, jump,
Thump, thump.
Help, I've fallen on my nose!
I must be brave
And must dare
To leap again
Through the air.
First, though I need my dinner
Before I grow much thinner,
I need to chew
But what can I do?
The acorns have gone with the tree,
Oh! what will become of me?
Please do not fear,
I'll survive, I'll keep alive,
And now I've a splendid idea.
I must bury an acorn below
So it can start to grow
Into another oak tree.
Its acorns you know
Won't have time to grow
For me, but my descendants you see,
Who'll live in Thomas' grandma's garden.

Margaret Nixon

The Somewhere Cottage

So many miles from here to there
In the land of Someday, Somewhere,
Sheltered safe in a distant vale,
Untouched by winter snow or hail,
Is a thatch-roofed cottage, small.
Near the door two fir trees tall.
One never hears the noisy planes
Or those rattling railway trains.

Lots of sunshine, bright blue sky,
Tiny clouds like white geese fly.
A lovely song when skylark sings
And butterflies with lilac wings.
Bees are busy around the flowers
As sun and shadows measure hours.
Collie dog sleeping on the green,
Puss waiting for a bowl of cream.

To freshen up the flowers bright
The rain falls only in the night.
A grey owl perches on the thatch,
Looking around for mice to catch.
In the cottage lives Sarah Leigh,
A sweet and smiling face has she.
'Early into bed and early to rise'
Is Sarah's motto, for she is wise.

She keeps her home shining clean
And looks after her garden green.
Once a week Sarah goes into town
In the village bus painted brown.
She owns a field and tiny stream,
And her cow gives milk and cream.
Old Cluckety Hen an egg does lay,
Just one for breakfast every day.

If by chance you should go there
To the land of Someday, Somewhere,
No other someone the secret tell
For you will break a magic spell.
Then the cottage and Sarah Leigh
Shall vanish away across the sea,
Taken by the old Witch Nevercare
Into the darkest land of Nowhere.

Cicely Goody

Fish Dish

Go and take the message,
Deliver it to the carp.
Bring me back an answer,
And play it on your harp.
You have to get to Dover,
And must trust your little sole.
Getting past the sharks and swordfish
Is now your ultimate goal.
Let me crab your attention,
And don't keep saying, 'Oh my cod!'
If you want to answer me
Just give a little nod.
'I'm urchin for a cup of tea,
Won't you have one too
Before you set out to depart
In the oceans blue?'
Don't forget you'll meet Mrs Haddock,
They all call her Fanny.
Except, of course her grandchildren,
Who obviously call her 'Nanny'.
Say hello to Mr Monkfish,
And ask him to bless your fins.
Also say you'd like him to
Forgive your many sins.
Ah yes, now there's Miss Octopus,
Who's always having kittens.
For out of the eight months of the twelve
She can never find her mittens.
Now when you return from your venture,
We'll have a bottle of wine.
Splash out on a party,
And have a real whale of a time.

Jane Shaer

Only Jesus

Only Jesus can cleanse us
Deep within
For sin has been inherited
In the hearts of men
We've all gone astray
And turned to our own way
This is why God sent His Son
To seek the lost
And for our sake went to the cross
So that we can have forgiveness
Be renewed in heart
But there is something that we
Have to do to be forgiven and be
Born anew
First we need to be conscious of sin
Humble ourselves
And come before Him
This great God of mercy
Is there for us all
And if we reach out
He'll come when we call
He knows all about us
And the things we have done
But if we ask Him, He'll pardon us
And forgive each one
He's the shepherd
Looking for lost sheep
And when He finds them
His joy is complete
All Heaven rejoices
In just one that's been found
For now we've been united with God
And Heaven bound

B Miller

With Reference To Being Like A Feather

The doctor said my emotions were like a feather.

Well, a feather . . . hah!
Well, I don't actually mind being a feather
and at the moment I am very much that.
There are advantages and disadvantages to being a feather
and I am a feather at the moment,
detached from a body
and do not know whether I am coming or going,
referring to my emotions being blown up and down, backwards
and forwards,

like many other feathers
I used to stuff a cushion and be slept on.

Feathers are also very strong and can take the most difficult of storms
and weather
carried across the sea on the ups and downs of waves.

It is, I suppose, all a matter of balance.
While all the feathers are attached to the body
there is security and progress and wholeness.
This is not always the case; sometimes the original body is all
we know,

the way we have been taught,
and is, unbeknown to us, a very dysfunctional body.

I don't actually believe that anyone is stupid;
we all, I can honestly say, believe in evil
and are so insecure and have detached ourselves from believing
there could be much good.
So okay, we can choose.
We either do or we don't choose to have a belief at all.
That's one decision we can make.
Have you ever heard the expression 'fight or flight',
trying to run before we have learned to walk?

Yes, I am a very dysfunctional,
damaged,
stuck-in-the-mud feather
and want to be attached to a body I believe in
and a body who believes in me,
that has faith in me and I also in the body.
Little feather, where is that faith?

In Christ, with all the other loose feathers.

Breda Brown

Last Mission

(Dedicated to the Royal Air Force. Per Ardua Ad Astra)

Slowly as they rose that night up into the air,
Off to give the enemy a trouncing in his lair.
A full load of twenty-five tons of bombs,
Well wrapped up against the cold for the journey was long.
The silent country below them as they approached the sea,
The white cliffs below, the last they'll see.

Navigator giving directions for their line of flight,
For they could see the landmarks on that moonlit night.
Approaching the enemy coastline, searchlights beamed aloft,
They knew that many shells were tossed.
Front and mid-upper gunner searching the sky,
Fighters were what they looked for up high.

Messerschmidt and Focke Wolf usually harried them,
On the way out they were thick and fast when,
On the way back they be waiting again,
No time to report or hold a pen.
Searchlights below and fighters above,
Made you think once more, those at home you love.

Down below was the battle zone so torn about,
Your own troops down there give the enemy a clout.
Coming up to the target zone soon must make ready,
Getting cold in here makes you feel so heady.
A whiff of oxygen to calm you down,
Thank goodness the target isn't another town.

A nice run in avoiding ack-ack shells,
Bombs gone now, yet of damage we can't tell.
Turn around and head for home and bed,
Flight plan laid to pilots, compass bearings read.
Through the fighters over the Channel
Landing strip ahead now time to unravel.

Lining up to go in, damn that fighter dodging in,
Crikey it's not ours, it's one of theirs.
Suddenly such a flash, a *bang!* We go up in smoke,
Bits and pieces fall to the ground.
Now all are gone, no more to fly,
They join the angels in the sky.
We will remember them.

Kenneth Copley

Reflections

Was I really worth it Lord?
Am I really worth it?
That you should die on Calvary's tree
For me, weak, sinful me
Was I really worth it?

All that pain, all that loss
Was I really worth it?
You thought so Lord
And to the temple daily went
With that intent, You must have thought me worth it.

Oh Lord I need You close at hand
As relationships hit the dust
There is no one else you see
Who will really care about me
Who makes me feel worthwhile.

First love yourself the books say
That's easier said than done
It's the temptation I deplore
Which comes knocking at my door
And to which I have succumbed.

To confess or not you see
The decision rests with me
No one else can make that choice
Whether I weep or whether rejoice.

I've always thought that honesty
Is the best policy
But sometimes not, I suspect
It places the problem on another neck.

So Lord I ask again, 'Am I really worth it?'
Is there anything I can do
Other than confess to You
Who will accept me as I am
Weakness, mistakes, all that I am
Am I worth it - really worth it?

Diana Blench

The Tamworth Two

This little piggy went to market
But two little piggies said no.
One little piggy was a very clever piggy
He said, 'I will say when we go.'
So at the top of the hill,
When all was still
He pushed his mate and said, 'Go, go, go,
The butchers will be sorry,
But it's not us they are going to swallow,
Not until we have seen some of the show.'
So up hill and down dale
These two little pigs did trail,
'We will stay free, just follow me.
So straighten your tail
Then they might lose the trail.
We will try to look like two dogs
Instead of two hogs.'
Then they laughed and squealed with glee,
'We are free, free, free.
All this walking will slim us down
And then we will look like two corkers
Instead of two porkers.'
As they passed by the farms and saw all
Their mates, they just thought how
Good life would be, if all animals were free.
'We love vegetarians don't we, we, we.'
After roaming all night and keeping out of sight
These two little piggies came across a wood.
The little pigs said,
'This looks good. If we make our home here
We will have nothing to fear,
No more will we have to roam.'
So please leave these little pigs alone,
Unless you can offer a better home.

K M Lockwood

Dad In A Million

Once Jesus told a parable
About a wasteful lad
Who wanted his inheritance
And said so to his dad
So Dad shared out his property
Between sons one and two
The younger son skedaddled off
To conquer pastures new
He squandered all his worldly wealth
Without a single qualm
His dosh ran out, then famine struck
Which caused him great alarm
He found employment tending pigs
Their food seemed such a feast
But not one bite was offered him
By man or porcine beast
Dejected, starving, full of woe
His thoughts went back to Dad
Whose workers all had food to spare
Life couldn't be too bad,
'I'm so unworthy,' sighed the lad,
'Not fit to be a son
I've sinned against my dad and God
Whatever can be done?
I'll have to go back home and plead
With Dad to take me on
And use me as an extra hand
All other rights have gone.'
So off he went, Dad saw him come
Excitement filled the air,
'I've let you down,' the lad announced
Dad didn't seem to care
He called his servants - 'Quick!' he yelled,
'Fetch robe and ring and shoe
My son was dead but now he lives
Let's kill the prize calf too!'
Big brother, hard at work, became
Aware of sounds of glee,

'There's something fishy going on
Whatever can it be?'
On finding out he took offence,
'That's charming, Dad!' raged he
'I've been a model son for years
You've never treated me!
That kid's hung out with prostitutes
And wasted all your cash
And yet you kill the fatted calf
You're being far too rash.'
'But son,' said Dad, 'what's mine is yours
I know you've stuck around
Be glad! This lad was dead but lives
Was lost but now is found.'

Helen M Clarke

Dolly

Till she died, the oldest of my friends,
took me to infants' school when she worked as a maid for my mum,
collected me at half-past three along with the headmistress'
complaints.

'But she is very strict,' my mum would be reminded.

Dolly knew all about strictness, past employers had guaranteed that -
fire blazing and hearth spotless by seven or else no breakfast;
wages docked for a broken saucer;
days off at Madam's discretion.
But better than the life at home,
the step-mother, the beatings.

By the time she came to us, she had a place of her own,
a room, rather, and paying part of her rent in housework,
the day-job running into the night-job.

Just occasionally, there was time and money for the music-hall,
a seat in the gods.
Next day we'd get a laugh-by-laugh commentary on the antics of
Dave Willis.

'He's so daft! He's lucky to be daft and get paid for it.
And we're lucky to have him to laugh at.'
She had no idea that someone could be professionally daft.
Just as well - would have killed the enchantment.

The music-hall became bingo (which she never took to),
Dolly became a pensioner, with the nearest yet to a place of her own -
a council flat.
She got a cat for company
and, when she realised that robberies were rife, a dog to protect her
with its barking.
She took in another cat, a stray - 'Before someone sells it to the labs.
It's awful what they do to the poor beasts!'
A neighbour, about to enter an old folks' home, couldn't bear to have
her dog put down.
Dolly to the rescue, refusing payment, 'Get away, five can live as
cheaply as four!'

When Dolly herself had to go that way, the council people must
have rounded up the animals,
but she said, 'No, I've still got them. They're out playing in the garden.
You'll see them crowding at the window soon. They always know when
it's teatime. My dad keeps an eye on them. He's got a job as the
gardener here.'
Then she asked, 'How's your mum? All right?'
'Oh - don't you remember? - She died many years ago.'
'No, she never!' Dolly dismissed this delusion of mine.
That exchange marked every visit
till at last I replied, 'Oh she's fine thank you.'
Once I added, 'She was asking for you,' and wondered at myself.

I was her one visitor, and only on holidays, for I had moved to a
                                                far-off town.
I would ring the home before I called . . . till
'Oh - I'm sorry to say Dolly is no longer with us.'
I'd missed her funeral by ten days.
I took flowers to the crematorium,
but there was no plaque or stone,
no place that was hers.
In the crematorium office, they said I could them in the Chapel of
Remembrance for one week only, then they'd be removed.
Yes, I was told, there had been some family at the funeral.
No, there had been no mention of a plaque.
They had no knowledge of the family,
I would have to ask the undertakers.
They gave a telephone number.

On which I explained that the deceased had been the oldest of my
friends and I would be glad to contribute to any memorial planned.
All they could do was forward a letter -
to which there was no reply.
Perhaps they took it the wrong way.

So that was Dolly.
Homes kept clean and running smoothly,
small kindnesses
(and, when she could, larger ones)
are not the stuff of obituaries.
This poem is the best I can do for Dolly.

Joe Solomon

Into The Fast Lane

The 1950s had a drab start, there was still rationing,
derelict bombsites, no housing room to spare,
but many nice reunions or memories to share.

A little boost came at Whitsun, the end of petrol rationing,
with dancing for joy on the forecourts, now holidays could begin.

Public transport mostly though, so few cars were made
these were sent for export to improve a desperate balance of trade.

So what excitement the Coronation, with the arrival of TV
and Edmund Hillary had reached the top of the world, a wonderful
place to be.

Then the sound barrier was broken, we were told that very soon
men would go up in rockets to look for the man in the moon.
For this was the dawn of the space age with great fulfilment's
to achieve
or will they find those little green men? There are people who
really believe.

Little did we know in a few years it would be so quick, the world to
travel round,
there would come a supersonic aircraft to travel twice the speed
of sound.

The fifties brought the first Eurovision Song Contest, Roger Banister
did the four minute mile
and Liberachi with his candelabra wore sequins and an
everlasting smile.

In 1959 came the first motorway, coffee bars, supermarkets too,
nylon, plastic, tights, mini skirts, the country had a whole new view,
Little children went to play school, watched Flowerpot Men and
Muffin the Mule,
Now children would be seen and heard, it was time to change
the rule.

People extended their houses to make some extra room,
there were bonnie children everywhere, the result of the baby boom.

There came a new word 'teenager' with rockers and teddy boys,
Bill Hayley visited England and brought an exciting noise.
We had our Tommy Steele, Cliff Richard, the Elvis Presley age,
The Beatles, The Monkees, Rolling Stones, the Billy Graham Crusade.

America's lovely sex symbol was Marilyn Monroe
with that 'Happy Birthday Mr President song, she really stole the show,
But in '63 the fateful day never to be forgot,
It was amid joy and jubilation that President Kennedy was shot.

Then came free love, flower power festivals, loud music blared from
sports cars,
top twenty records, women's lib when ladies burnt their bras.

Now with this decade ended it was time to turn the page
and move into the fast lane to greet the electronic age.

June Dixon

The Portrait

I see you there, you seem so real,
I long to stroke your hair.
The smile that lights your dear, dear face
And crinkles your eyes as they shine
With your mischievous laughter.
My dear, why? . . . Why did you have to go?

Leaving me here so empty and alone
Without you. Not for us
To wonder why, tis for us to do or die . . .
I wonder who wrote those words and why?

That's just what you had to do my love,
You had to die,
But we know there is no death.
So what now? You are there and I'm still here
And all we were, all we dreamed
Has no meaning without you to share.

I found the photo, the portrait
As I sorted through your papers.
It was so 'you' darling and I set it into a frame
Opposite my cosy chair
Where I can sit, gaze and remember.

So real, so out of reach -
I need to touch your cheek with mine
And feel warmth of you as I used to do.
I need the strength of you,
My rock and hiding place.

But you are not there,
Only the cold glass of the frame.
Those hands rested on my shoulders
And I can remember their power
When the photo was taken.
Now they stay behind the glass
And I am bereft of their strength.

I am not angry that you have gone from me.
We both knew the score - the time had come
When one of us must move on, and one
Remain to complete the work undone.

Now at least you are free from pain
And one day we will be together again.

But I am hurting here inside.
No day has passed that I've not cried.
Our love was strong and despite the world
We balanced well and our love was true.

And yet . . . and yet . . . I cannot bear
I can no longer stroke your hair!
The little things that mean so much,
Just being here, your tender touch.
The way you understood
In times I thought you never would.
I miss you now so very much.

So I must face the world alone,
Although I'm blessed in many ways -
Loving family, friends and God.
Without all these I could not be
And I must shed the selfish me,
Let you go on to a new life, my soulmate!
Happy I was once your wife.

Some day when the mists have gone,
Together we may still go on.
Hand in hand through sunshine's blaze . . .
Beyond the earthly life's sad ways
To live our truth and honour love.
Two souls becoming one God's love.

Hazel Brydon

The Lifeboat

In her proud colours
of orange and blue
she stands on the slipway
awaiting her crew.

She follows with pride
the Solomon Browne
her forerunner known worldwide
as the Pride of Penlee.

Eight strong men that December night
answered the call
to save the stricken coaster
the ill-fated Union Star.

Time and again they tried
their efforts to be thwarted
as the cruel sea drove them apart
bowed but undaunted.

Those courageous men
refused to give in
they would try once again
but sadly it wasn't to be.

Those giant waves
tossed them aside
then threw the doomed coaster
on top of the Penlee.

The unthinkable happened that dark awful night
the lifeboat was lost.
Gone too the poor souls on the Union Star
those brave men had fought their last fight.

The village of Mousehole
will never forget
the crew of the lifeboat
that never came back.

But now she stands ready and waiting
for the youngest coxswain in the RNLI
Neil Brockman, son of Nigel
crewman on the Solomon Browne.

Here comes the call
her crew come running
down the slipway she falls
the Mable Alice, the new Pride of Penlee.

Lydia Stanton

The Widow's Tale

(After Chaucer - the first tale on the walk along the SW coast)

In Somerset, a mile from Minehead town
A ford allows a stream to tumble down,
To flood the fields and onward to the seas.
Beyond the ford, but hidden by the trees
An ancient farmhouse nestles in the dell
And it's God's truth that I'm about to tell.

There was a farmer lived there years gone by.
He was not true, no he was really sly.
Drunkenness he portrayed both day and night.
Unwary travellers soon ran off in fright.
He cursed, blasphemed and threatened with his knife.
His hollow laughter terrified his wife.
She trembled, wept and prayed it was that day
The smugglers came; with her beloved Ray.

Those Exmoor fields sloped down to meet the sea,
Where tide-rip waters could not hold a quay.
But west of them the sea had formed a bay,
A sandy shore - it can be seen today.
In raging storms the sea did more. The waves,
Had carved within the sandstone hills two caves.
The smugglers came there when the night was dark,
Sebastian, Raymond and roughneck Mark.

What was the contraband? You may well ask.
Golden liquid matured within the cask.
Cognac. This smoothing drink we sip today,
The prince of drinks. I give it my hurray.

But hush, on that black night in early May
The honest townsfolk slept a mile away.
Only the farmer and his wife could see
The stealthy, silent work of smugglers three.

The work was done when Mark went to the farm.
He and the farmer met without alarm.
They ate, they talked and drank the golden brew.
When in their cups, the wife went to the crew.
She took wild rabbit stew, infused with dill,
Along the path beneath that Exmoor Hill.
Her eyes were bright, her cheeks were burning red,
Her heart beat fast. She'd soon be in his bed.

The smugglers' caves were deep, high, warm and clean.
Sebastian shared his with young Eileen.
Raymond's was ready for the farmer's wife.
That night would be remembered all her life.
Outside the caves on that dark balmy night
Four lovers ate the stew, with great delight,
They washed it down with water from the stream.

Two pairs of lovers, stirred as in a dream,
To go within their chosen caves. But, we
Cannot follow. It's not for us to see.
All passions spent - a silence filled the bay.
The lovers slept without a thought of day.

The farmer called his wife to bring them bread.
He searched the farm, but found that she had fled.
His drunken rage was really quite obscene.
He swore, he cursed. Again he showed his spleen.
Mark mimicked this display of rage; but smiled.
His plan had been to get the farmer riled.
He aimed to have that farm as his own home.
His plans were laid. No longer would he roam.

The raging pair went out along the shore
To find the crew, and hear if they knew more
About the missing wife. Mark held his breath.
A noise could speed the drunken farmer's death . . .
But not from Mark. The farmer must invade
The silence of that night. Yes, his tirade
Would call forth members of the crew - to kill
Then Mark would live beneath that Exmoor hill.
The plan went well. The farmer cursed and swore.
Silence was broken, more and more and more.

The farmer's wife and young Eileen still lay
Asleep, within the caves south of the bay.
Sebastian and Raymond grasped their knives.
They were prepared to sacrifice their lives.
Guard the contraband was what Mark had said.
No time to question who was out of bed.
The knives went into both the drunken men.
They had no time to say their last Amen.

The farmer's widow whispered, 'Come with me.
The farm is warm. There's no one here to see
Who did these dreadful killings in the bay.
The tide will rise and take the men away.'

Two pairs of lovers lived within that farm.
Their lives were full and no one came to harm.

The years have passed, new owners live there now.
They love the farm, so I will take my bow.
But should you go there in the early May,
You'll find two drunkards roaming in the bay.
Each year they're searching for the crew.
They cannot see you. Treat them as a joke.
Ghosts cannot harm God-fearing honest folk.

Come sip with me this princely drink - cognac.
Then all of us can go and hit the sack.

Evelyn Golding

The Incas Of Peru

Low beneath the quiet mountain
   Sleeping silently in snow
Where the only living creatures
   Are the grey short-sighted fruit bats
Once there was a race of people
   Tall and straight and beautiful,
And their wild black hair was braided
   With the vivid peacock's feathers.
Children of the Sun were they
   And the sun gave them its colour.
Long limbed women sang gay love songs
   As they decked their flowered tables
With the plump round fruits of autumn.
   Where the golden platters glistened,
Crimson wine in agate beakers
   Winked with laughing rosy bubbles.
Jewels sparkled in their daggers,
   Rich blood ruby, glowing topaz,
Great square emeralds, yellow quartz rock
   Hewn in strange shapes for their children.
Now the Incas are a legend,
   Wither went they in their laughter?
Gone the songs, their lips are flowers
   Growing in the rocky crevice.
Gold has gone save where the sunlight
   Glimmers on the rounded pebbles
In the quickening mountain streamlets.
   Gone the jewels from their daggers
Heavy goblets set with sapphires
   Lapis Lazuli in pendants
And the dewy chrysolite.
   Many people seek their treasures
Many die in wanton craving
   But the fiery Inca curses
Seal the jewels in the mountains
   Low beneath the tired Andes
Sleeping silently in snow.

Olga M Momcilovic

Divorce

What is divorce?
It is the separation of two minds,
The departure of one soul from another.
It is the hardest decision to make,
As from each heart, time will take
The love that once was there.

It is hard to believe all the feelings
That come and go! Where?
Not to be shared with each other,
So maybe a sister or brother?
No! It seems not. You're on your own.
Left to examine those feelings.

Feelings of regret, as you ask, 'Why?'
Doubt, as you ponder, *should I*?
Sadness, when the answer is *yes!*
Anger! When words of blame are bantered about.
Sorrow! When family shut you out!
Confusion, as one asks, 'Who did what? Said this, did that?'

Deep pain as the reality becomes clear -
The death of your marriage is finally here.
A sense of grief as you mourn your loss.
You try to act naturally, as if you don't give a toss,
But one's eyes tell the truth, show the depression that's hidden
Time for confession. Reconciliation? - Not a chance.

So let's go to the pub, get drunk and dance!
No! That doesn't solve the problem.
All you can do is . . . what? Still love them?
Then the truth dawns - you have lost them all -
Husband, daughters, sons, grandchildren too.
What is divorce? It's a living Hell -
And I don't know what to do!

Tears flow, day and night,
You question your motives. Did I do right?
Should I have hung on? Would things have got better?
You tell yourself, 'No!' as your pillow gets wetter.
So you tuck your heart away, vowing never to love again.
And just pray that time will heal the pain.
That's what divorce is.

Maureen Newman

The Home Help Brigade

For years and years I've been a 'Home Help',
I've tramped around what seems a thousand miles,
To render some assistance to the those who need it, kind,
I've done my best to please, and my loyalty to equally divide,
Up to the neck in snow I've been and soaked to the skin.
But my sense of humour never faltered,
I could still offer a cheerful, 'Good morning madam. Are you ill?'
She'd look at me and say, 'Oh it's someone new,
I haven't had you before, what do I call you?'

'Well I hope you will accept me and take me as I am.'
Just as I said this, her door closed with a slam.
When I'd finished all the chores, she's stood full of praise,
'Oh I do hope you'll come again, and on all the other days.'

Off I go to my next call, the same old tale again,
To hear a different story, is almost all in vain,
Washing, scrubbing, polishing, shopping,
It's all in a days work and certainly keeps you hopping,
Worn out and weary and clean fed up.
You hope your feet will carry you to the nearest,
Gone as usual, bloody bus!

My working days are nearly over,
It had to come alas,
I'll have to hang my nose-bag up,
And be turned out to grass.
But as sure as Heaven's above
If I don't retire soon,
I'll be blasted into orbit,
To be a 'Home Help' to a client
Living somewhere on the moon.

Isabel Kelly

A Fusilier's Pain

At seventeen when life's just beginning
A normal young lad without a limb missing
Joining the army, to go see the world
Instead saw the horrors, now to be told
From the sands of the desert
To the rocks of Aden
Crater so filthy, so black, heavy laden
Its people so filled with hatred
For the peace-keepers there
Observing from cliffs high up above
Those who lie far below
Those who scheme in the darkness
To kill the young men who watch from the hill
Unaware of the terror that waits down below
The men of Northumberland
With caution tread
Aware of the people who watch and who stare
They would kill at a glance
And leave our bones bare
On twentieth of June fate showed its face
To the young men in Crater on that fatal day
Outnumbered and ambushed
By the evil that waits
No quarter was given
To the men stranded there
Those butchers of Aden
Left no one in doubt
That the brave souls who went there
Would never come out
Bodies all broken, lying around
No solace for the men who fell to the ground
In a place far from home, together they lie
In a valley so silent, so lonely and bare
Now at peace they will rest
The pain hurts no more
My thoughts always with them
By night and by day
I'm proud to have served with them
On that fateful day.

Jim Keightley

Blitzed Out In Blaris

I remember that evening like it was only yesterday when I had to
evacuate Belfast,
That warm spring afternoon, way back in 1943, when those bombs
rained down,
I'd only just got to Mrs McCrorry's little shop to buy a bag of sweets
and a comic,
As I was leaving the shop, I was thrown into the air as the bombs
crashed down,
However, two streets away which is where I lived, people weren't as
lucky as I was.
I returned to find our house had been flattened but luckily Mum and
Dad were fine,
Father had his arm around Mother to comfort her, as tears streamed
down her face,
Everything apart from their wedding photograph had been destroyed
in a few minutes.
She thanked the Lord that I was still alive, when she spotted me
a few yards away.

We had a choice to make, we could either spend the evening in the
local Orange Hall,
Or else head for the safety of the countryside, by walking for miles
along the towpath,
My parents weren't going to risk the chance of more bombs being
dropped during the night,
Also there was nothing for us now in our little street, which had been
wiped out,
We decided to leave Belfast for the peace and quiet of the rambling
countryside,
At least sleeping in a field was a much safer option than being sitting
ducks in a hall!

We walked that dusty towpath, as narrowboats drifted by, pulled by
huge horses,
Their tails swayed in the breeze and the man aboard tipped his hat
and smiled at us,
I thought he should've offered us a lift, as my poor feet had begun
to get blisters,
I was also very hungry as my bag of sweets had finished, soon as
we'd begun our trip,

All I wanted to do was to go to sleep in a haystack with Mum and
Dad to comfort me,
When suddenly we spotted a lady with two children, waving a
gaslight towards us,
She welcomed us into her home with open arms and so we
followed her.

This lady lived in a small house, affectionately known locally as the
'Lockhouse',
She lived there with her children, Billy and June and her husband
who entertained us,
He would start to sing like Frankie Vaughan once he drank the
cooking sherry,
There was a pot of vegetable soup on the stove and we became
honoured guests,
As I sat outside with my friends and I could still hear bombs
being dropped,
This humble family had been our saviours during that spring of 1943.

Years later, after the war ended, I used to visit that family, as I never
forgot their generosity or how they took us in as part of their family,
for that one night.

Ben E Corado

Blitz's Child

The war is just beginning and everything
is changed.
Grandad's digging up the garden
and Granny has a pain.

But the doctors have gone away
to help the men at war,
So Granny takes the ov'r counter stuff
and stares at the door.

Mummy thumbs a recipe,
anything with Spam!
It's all about 'making do or mend',
we don't really need the pan.

Daddy's best suit hangs on guard
a' back of the bedroom door.
And I can hear sweet sorrow's cries
of a love, Mum's wishing for.

In the night, it's very dark
when all the lights have gone.
It's as if the world's asleep
and then the nightmares come along.

A siren wails its pain thro' air,
then a plane spits its mal de mer.
Huddled under boxes stuck with sticky tape,
it's a wonder we survived at all, squeezed behind my cape.

'Never mind the hardships,' my grandad said one day,
'we all work together and we're sure to find a way.
Justice will prevail and the war will cease to be.'
I was never in any doubt my dad would come home to me.

When 'All Clear' has sounded off, I always feel a dread,
cos now we all return to find nothing but a bed.
There's nothing but a doorpost and hinges standing firm.
No home or garden, just that funny bottle Mum used
when she got that perm.

Different things are important now. Your coupons and your box.
The one tied over your shoulder in case the gas stuff is aloft.
No one bothers about homework or if you keep a book,
but never try to nick a ham off the butcher's hook.

Everybody's working and girls are digging pits,
there are ladies in men's clothing,
Odd, cos nothing fits!
But there's always the cinema with its starry life galore.
With film and news designed to cheer and leave you
wanting more!

And now the whole thing's over
the memories are paged away.
Will the tears of yesterday
wet the fears of today?

Kim Taylor

I Remember It Well

I remember one September when I was just fourteen,
Everything white was camouflaged to different shades of green,
Chamberlain said, 'I do regret this country is at war!'
Soldiers with bayonets by barricades stood on guard around
our shores.

Children were evacuated to different country places,
They were sad to leave their homes and arrived with tear-stained faces
Women brought up families alone, for husbands they were without,
Fathers were just photographs, children were told about.

I remember the forces, all marching on parade,
We called out, 'God bless you!' how we cheered and waved,
We thought it was marvellous to see them all so smart,
Our young minds didn't realise what horror was to start.

I remember Eisenhower, Montgomery and Churchill,
How with his great speeches, gave us all the will
To carry on through thick and thin
When the darkest days of war looked so very grim.

I remember clothes and food all went on the ration,
Land Girls were brought in to help feed the nation,
Women took on men's jobs so they could go to war,
Men died in their thousands in the air and on the shore.

I remember the Desert Rats and the brave Burma men,
The blackout, the buzz bombs and Air Raid Wardens,
Nurses were like angels - tending wounded on front lines,
Many sailors drowned when their ships were sunk by mines.

By 1943 I had left school behind,
I was now a young woman with a sweetheart on my mind,
Lots of sweethearts married on a 48 hour leave,
Women were left with babies and all too soon, bereaved.

I remember the Americans arriving with their jeeps,
They gave the grown-ups cigarettes and the children sweets,
We were very glad to have them fighting on our side,
Many fell in love with the English girls, who became GI Brides.

I remember the convoys when D-Day was getting near,
The wailing of the sirens and waiting for the All Clear,
We used to count the bombers as they flew out overhead,
When they returned, we counted and knew many more were dead.

I remember VE Day, the people all went wild,
The king and queen waved from the balcony,
Not everybody smiled.
For their were many widows who sat alone and cried.
No one is a winner when fighting a war,
Both sides lost people they loved and cared for.
When the poppies fall in the Albert Hall,
I remember them all.

Mollie Carter

Troubadour

(For the many innocent victims of conflict worldwide, who are not remembered)

Troubadour, Troubadour
Where have you been?
To a thousand lands eyes have not seen.

Troubadour, Troubadour
What did you do there?
I played a sad song and uttered a prayer.
I have seen blood pour.
I have seen tears run.
I have seen evil's core.
Heard death's drum.
While the world shuts its eyes
And turns away
I continue wandering from day to day.

Troubadour, Troubadour
Do I see you cry?
The tears are all gone my child
The sun depicts a lie.

Troubadour, Troubadour
Why do you sing once more?
My songs are saved for dying breaths
Those we do ignore.
I sing for those who have no voice
Nothing left to mend.
I sing for their sorrow.
I sing for their end.

Troubadour, Troubadour
Why are you here?
The world has stopped its watching
Can't you smell the fear?

Troubadour, Troubadour
Please tell me what you mean.
The hungry are now starving.
The machetes now do glean.
Evil is growing daily
While the world hides away.
I will sing for your sorrow
I will help you pray

I will lift my voice
When other voices fail
Listen child to the powerful song
Not the piercing wail.

Troubadour, Troubadour
How long will you sing?
Until there is justice
An end to suffering.

Troubadour, Troubadour
Where do you go?
It is the end my child
But look at the glow.
Heaven is waiting.
Peace and restoration.
Remember what I say
I will see you one day
For now I must depart
Oh it breaks my heart
But there are lands that have no voice.
I have no choice.

Sabrina Mahtani

Regiments Of Ghosts (Part 2)

I walk through the millions of poppy flowers
seeds were scattered on sacred ground in the silent hours
it seems each scented poppy is for each man that fell
I can feel their fears . . . fears that they cannot now tell.

I can hear the artillery shells fall a thousand yards away
I can see the midnight sky light up like a firework display
I can feel the heat on my face as I stare over the trench
I can smell the acrid smoke and the burning stench.

I sink down in the trench, I cannot believe the scene
maybe in a moment if I blink it will be just a dream
tears form in my eyes from the smoke and mist
I tremble with fear, without hope, without a wish.

My heart races fast but does not skip a beat
my whole body is shaking from my head to my feet
my mind is spinning from the noise of the blasts
and I can hear myself crying, crying for my past.

'Oh I want to be back in the green pastures of England
without the 'King's shilling' in my hand.
I want to be walking in the dales of my home shire
with a burning heart for the love I so desire.'

'Hush,' the sergeant whispers, 'hush my bonnie lad
for you look like the son I never had.'
He puts his arm around my shoulder to bring me near
he does not seem to tremble, as he draws from me my fear.

I look him in the eye and not a tear can I see
no emotion, but a passion to fight, and to be free.
With a nod of his head, his lips begin to smile,
'Come on bonnie lad, together we will go this one last mile.'

I look around at my comrades as we prepare to advance
their bodies are still, their minds captured in a trance
suddenly the general's cry goes out, a whistle sounds
then mass confusion and the sergeant cannot be found.

Over the trench I go and into the depths of the unknown
running forward among men that have fallen, some still groan
deafening explosions all around, then shrapnel pierces my heart
I sink to my knees wondering, *how did all this madness start?*

I hear my father saying, 'God speed my son, time for you to sleep.'
I feel my mother's love, like the shrapnel, her love is so deep.

Jeff Milburn

Seven/Seven

Early morning
A summer's day
People commuting
Going on their way
A deal to be settled
A new dress to buy
A plane to be caught
An audition to try
The bus on the street
The train underground
A new day in the city
Has just begun -

Blinding flash . . .
Blast . . .
Shuddering halt . . .
Dark, eerie silence
Confusion, terror
Blackened faces, frightened eyes
Shouting, screaming
Shrill cries of suffering
Choking smoke, searing heat
Twisted metal grinding
Shattered glass shearing
Broken bodies, broken lives
Pain, agony, people dying
Bewilderment
Disbelief . . . !

Early morning
A summer's day
Commuters undaunted
Going on their way
A point to be made
A need to be strong
People of courage
Righting the wrong

Putting behind
The sorrow and pain
The great British spirit
Triumphs again.

J M Waine

Knowledge

God picked up a handful of dust,
From his perfect world,
And breathed life upon it.
The dust took form, became 'Adam'
And he was as perfect as the dust
From which he came.
Although . . .
Something was wrong with the mix -
Of breath and dust -
Maybe a few particles went astray
For Adam was lonely,
Despite God's care and a perfect world,
So God took Adam's rib to make 'Eve'.
Maybe God understood the solitude of Adam;
Maybe that was why He made the angels and Adam;
So that even He would not be alone.
But . . .
When God makes such things,
He makes only mirror images.
He knows the awesomeness of power,
Knows it is too much for His creations to bear.
Lucifer, God's favourite angel,
Led Adam, God's favourite creation, to rebel.
So God let both man and angel know
A little of the horror of knowledge.
Man separated-divided -
Became many colours with many beliefs,
All of these based on the scraps of knowledge from God.
Complete . . .
Knowledge is God, but
Fragmented, knowledge becomes
Prejudice and bigotry and, ultimately, hate.
And all of man's fragmented knowledge
Will never cement with that of the Devil's
Into a 'theory of everything'.
A knowledge that is God.

And . . .
As we live and progress in our
Pools of isolation
We want to flow together, coagulate, to become one man;
A part of the whole world and God.
But . . .
No matter how we try or
What we achieve -
Good or evil -
It is only when we die and dissolve into dust
That we become part of the world.
And for a near eternity we will wait as dust.
For a near eternity,
Be the ground beneath the feet of fools such as us
Hoping . . .
God will use his breath again so that we can
Prove worthy of creation.

Tim Cully

Country Life 1938 - 1946

The year was 1944. The country was at war.
My dad had built a bungalow and Grandma lived next door.
A tiny village called 'Lane End' was peace at such a time,
Wild roses and fields of cornflowers adorned the countryside.
Houses, a pub, farm and school, divided by a common;
Threepence bought a jug of milk. To the farm, I walked quite often.
I watched the farmer milk the cows and butter being churned.
Sometimes a free bag of cherries, much yearned.
I heard lads whistling one sunny day,
Beyond the school, I could see the hard labour
As they pitch fork hay.
Dad would wake me early to pick mushrooms in the field,
We then strolled home to show Mum, proud of our yield.
At the village hall, a film was shown - sheer terror,
My very first time. A train speeding towards
'The Dead-End Kids', strapped to a railway line.
We welcomed two evacuees and cousins came to stay,
Lots of animals to play with, to pass the time of day.
Home-made jam and bread, free range eggs, organic veg,
Milk puddings and caraway seed cake.
Tea with Grandma was such a treat, all this tasty food to eat.
When the Queen of Albania came to stay,
I was chosen to curtsy with a bouquet.
A photo was taken, which I still have today.
What a wonderful start in life, for my brother and me,
To play close to the earth, and feel totally free.

Janey Wiggins

Anchor Books Information

We hope you have enjoyed reading this book - and that you will continue to enjoy it in the coming years.

If you like reading and writing poetry drop us a line, or give us a call, and we'll send you a free information pack.

Alternatively if you would like to order further copies of this book or any of our other titles, then please give us a call or log onto our website at www.forwardpress.co.uk

Anchor Books Information
Remus House
Coltsfoot Drive
Peterborough
PE2 9JX

(01733) 898102